THE MORALITY OF GROUPS

SOUNDINGS

A Series of Books on Ethics, Economics, and Business

THOMAS DONALDSON, EDITOR

The Morality of Groups:

Collective Responsibility, Group-Based Harm, and Corporate Rights

LARRY MAY

University of Notre Dame Press
Notre Dame, Indiana

The author and publisher gratefully acknowledge permission to reprint, in revised form, articles which originally appeared in the following journals:

Ohio State Law Journal for portions of "Litigating Against Poverty," copyright © 1984 Ohio State University.

Philosophical Studies for "Vicarious Agency and Corporate Responsibility," which appeared in volume 43 (1983), pp. 69-82.

Social Theory and Practice for "Harming Women as a Group," which appeared in volume 11, number 2 (summer 1985).

Journal of Business Ethics for "Corporate Property Rights," which appeared in volume 5, number 3 (June 1986), pp. 225-232, copyright © 1986 D. Reidel Publishing Company.

Library of Congress Cataloging-in-Publication Data

May, Larry.
    The morality of groups.

    (Soundings)
    Includes index.
    1. Social ethics. 2. Social groups—Moral and ethical aspects. 3. Law—Philosophy. 4. Business ethics.
I. Title. 2. Series: Soundings (Notre Dame, Ind.)
HM216.M315   1987   302.3   87-40350
ISBN 0-268-01366-7

Manufactured in the United States of America

FOR MY PARENTS

Contents

SOUNDINGS

A Series of Books on Ethics, Economics, and Business

The Morality of Groups inaugurates a new series of books by the University of Notre Dame Press on the topic of ethics, economics, and business. The series, called SOUNDINGS, will publish high quality, book-length analyses of social and moral issues involving business or economics. SOUNDINGS was inspired by the perception of a dearth of scholarly writings existing in an area whose rapid rise has produced a bounty of textbooks and other teaching tools.

SOUNDINGS is committed to the idea that the research of business values must be either interdisciplinary or multidisciplinary: that is, it must either mix disciplinary approaches in a single analysis or contain within itself a variety of individual analyses, each one of which utilizes a distinct disciplinary base. Hence, the series will offer works presented from the perspectives of social science, philosophy, economics, theology, business, political science, and public policy.

Thomas Donaldson
Editor, SOUNDINGS
Loyola University of Chicago

Acknowledgments

Three years ago, shortly after receiving tenure, several of my colleagues convinced me, based partially on the assessment of my previous work by outside reviewers, that a book project on collective responsibility and harm should be my next task. I am especially grateful to Bill McBride who first helped me see how much of such a book I had already written in the midst of various papers in philosophy of law and business ethics. The entire manuscript was read in first draft by Rod Bertolet, and he encouraged me tremendously through his sympathetic reading of the text. Nani Ranken also read most of this first draft, and fought with me paragraph by paragraph, greatly enriching the book. I also received important criticism from Manfred Kuehn, Cal Schrag, and again from Bill McBride. Finishing the book would have surely taken several additional years if Purdue University had not provided me a sabbatical during which I did little else but work on the book.

Various parts of this book are greatly revised versions of papers I have previously published. Several of these papers were originally co-authored. I am most grateful to John Hughes and Marie Failinger for their assistance in first thinking through several issues in the book. My greatest debt incurred in writing this book is to Marilyn Friedman for allowing me to use parts of three of our co-authored papers. Together these papers constitute the bulk of chapter six. Marilyn also read successive drafts of the central chapters of the book, and, as always, provided more constructive criticism than I could effectively use.

I am grateful to the following journals for allowing me to reprint material of mine from their journals: *The Ohio State Law Journal*, *Philosophical Studies*, *Social Theory and Practice*, and *The Journal of Business Ethics*. I am also grateful to have had the opportunity to read various versions of these chapters to: The Sartre Society, The Society for

Business Ethics, The North American Society for Social Philosophy, The Society for Philosophy and Public Affairs, and the Eighth Annual Applied Philosophy Conference at Bowling Green State University, as well as several eastern division meetings of the American Philosophical Association. I wish to thank, collectively, all those who commented on my work at those meetings.

Peter French read the penultimate version of the manuscript and provided me with a very detailed critique. Thomas Donaldson provided many critical comments on this version and also went through the manuscript line-by-line with stylistic suggestions. I owe a special debt of gratitude to Tom, the editor of a new series of books at Notre Dame, for encouraging me from the beginning and for choosing my book as the first in this series. I also thank Carole Roos and John Ehmann for their help in the final editing.

Introduction

This book will attempt to fill a gap in contemporary ethics by presenting a systematic investigation of the status of groups in ethical theory. The vast majority of essays in contemporary ethics concerns the analysis of individual acts of discrete, and often socially isolated, individual persons. There are two major exceptions to this generalization. First, some philosophers working in decision theory have recently become interested in n-person prisoner's dilemmas, in which groups of persons face hard choices and must decide on the optimal strategy to pursue. Second, other philosophers working in applied ethics have become increasingly aware of the importance of groups such as corporations, nation states, and health care teams in the attempt to assess social policy in the fields of business, government, and medicine. But both decision theorists and applied ethicists have generally not provided a comprehensive understanding of how morality relates to social groups. In attempting to meet this challenge I will first examine the ontological and moral status of the nature (chapter one), action (chapter two), and intentions (chapter three) of social groups. Then I will examine the relationship between individual and group concepts of responsibility (chapter four), interest (chapter five), and harm (chapter six). Finally, I will conclude with a lengthy chapter on the justice of group-oriented political and legal strategies (chapter seven).

In 1978 I first became interested in the ethics of group behavior when I was consulted about a lawsuit being brought against Yale University for sexual harassment. Given that sexual harassment is an act perpetrated by one individual person against another, could an institution such as a university be legally responsible for such an act? Clearly, the whole group of members of the university had not engaged in the harassment of the female student who was bringing the complaint. Did this mean that the university, seen as a group of individuals, only some of whom engaged in harassing practices, could

1

not be plausibly said to be responsible for the sexual harassment? From these questions I was led to more general philosophical questions about the nature of collective action and responsibility.[1]

This case illustrates the difficulty which moral theorists and legal practitioners have had when they have applied individualistic notions of action and responsibility to groups of persons. The insight I formed in analyzing the case was that the structure of the group was crucial in any moral appraisal of the behavior of social groups. The way that a professor's job was described and the way in which other job-holders within the university hierarchy were authorized to respond to complaints made against professors seemed very relevant to whether this professor could have, or would have, engaged in the harmful conduct at all. The structure of this social group established special privileges and duties which themselves were instrumental in facilitating the harm. Because of these considerations, I concluded that in this and similar cases it does make sense to hold the university responsible for what had occurred.

Corporations and mobs, nation states and teams, professional associations and jazz quartets are all social groups. Each is a collection of individual persons related in such a way that the group can engage in collective action or can be acted upon as a group. By "collective action" I mean that group members aid one another in significant ways and thereby enable other members to act differently than they could act on their own. In some cases people are literally able to *do* things in groups they couldn't do alone. In other cases, the effect of what individuals do, or the description of those acts, is different when the individuals are members of social groups. And in yet other cases, even when collective action does not occur, it may be that people will be acted upon quite differently as members of groups than if these same people were not members.

Yet, in contemporary ethical theory, social groups are generally not subjected to special conceptual investigation. Rather, we find such philosophers as John Rawls blithely claiming that what holds true for the justice of *persons* participating in a practice will also hold true for nations and businesses.[2] I readily admit that social groups *can* be treated *as if* they were individual persons. But, the question I wish to address is this: Which way of conceptualizing social groups best fits the data of experience (from sociology, psychology, law, political science, etc.) in contemporary times?

The thesis of this book is that the *structure* of social groups plays such an important role in the acts, intentions, and interests of members of groups, that social groups should be given a moral status different from that of the discrete individual persons who compose them. Thus, the chief target of this book is the thesis that the moral standing of social groups is no different from the aggregate moral standing of individual, isolated persons. But I am also critical of those theorists who see the social group as having a moral standing completely separate from the discrete individual persons who constitute the group. The structure of a social group is the set of relationships that exist among the group's members. While these relationships make for different acts, intentions, and interests than would exist outside the group, nonetheless they are relationships *of* individual persons.

Throughout this book, I argue that social groups should be morally evaluated by carefully examining the group structures through which individual members of the group are related to each other. Such a thesis, if established, calls for a major change in the way in which ethical theory is investigated. A large part of our books and courses in ethical theory should be devoted to subjects and concepts that are wider in scope than the personal actions, intentions, and interests of individual actors.

My approach throughout will be to work with those moral concepts about which there is at least some agreement when applied to individual persons. I will show what adaptations are needed in these moral conceptions when a group rather than an individual is acting or being acted upon. Of course, this means that the initial chapters must establish in what ways it does make sense to talk of a social group as if it were a moral agent. In these chapters, and those that follow, I will stick to examples drawn from social science and literature, rather than the highly artificial examples which are still widespread in certain ethical discussions.

After viewing the adaptations of current moral concepts needed to deal with the actions and harms of social groups, one may be tempted to urge a more radical restructuring of ethical theory than that presented here. I do not advocate such major changes in our ethical concepts for two reasons. First, it will emerge in what follows that our standard moral conceptions, with appropriate modification, allow us to make sense out of a wide range of group experience. Here, as elsewhere, different conceptual schemes should be tested by their adequacy to make sense of the world. Second, there is a close connection between moral and legal conceptions. If one overturns a set of moral conceptions it is quite likely to cause the overturning of the corresponding set of legal conceptions as well. And while I believe that there are many things wrong with contemporary legal conceptions of harm, responsibility, and rights, it would be a mistake to abandon completely these time-tested conceptual schemes.

The issues taken up in this book are not new. Plato spends a great deal of time in *The Republic* talking about the ethics of the city-state. From Plato's time to the present, many philosophers have taken up the relation between the individual and group in political communities. Hobbes, Locke, and Rousseau wrote extensively on government and the family. They wrote only a bit about small-scale companies and mobs, but none of this analysis was directed at institutions and organizations of the sort most of us encounter everyday: business corporations, medical institutions, and professional associations. I will occasionally draw on the historical tradition in moral and political philosophy to aid in understanding the various issues of this book. However, the type of analysis in this book did not and perhaps could not occur prior to the rise of large-scale social groups, such as corporations, which are today often more influential than the political institutions which consumed the attention of previous moral philosophers.

From the turn of the century until the 1950s there was a rich literature in philosophy of social science on the relation between the individual and society. As will be most obvious from chapter one, this literature has had an impact on my own deliberations. Indeed, it is to this literature that I will first turn in attempting to grasp the ontological status of the social group. But this literature did not often progress into the realm of ethical theory, since most of these philosophers believed, with the members of the Vienna Circle, that normative inquiry had no place in philosophy.

The vast majority of work in contemporary ethics has tended to skirt rather than confront the questions I will address here, but there are exceptions to this generalization, and I will draw heavily on these works. Philosophers such as Joel Feinberg, Richard De-George, Virginia Held, and Peter French have taken groups seriously enough to write major essays on the subjects of collective action and responsibility. The greatest work to date on the status of groups in social philosophy is Jean-Paul Sartre's *Critique of Dialectical Reason*,[3] a work often not appreciated in Anglo-American philosophy. Unfortunately, Sartre is only tangentially interested in the status of groups in moral philosophy, displaying a typical continental bias against ethical controversies.

I have been strongly influenced by the recent empirical work in sociology, psychology, and organizational theory on social groups, and will refer to this body of research often. Other applied ethicists are also currently trying to make sense of empirical research concerning groups in business and medicine. But the diversity of disciplines and fields of inquiry under investigation has made it difficult for applied ethicists to find the time to step back and survey the entirety of the field to discover common metaphysical and moral difficulties.

In the remainder of this introduction, I will set out the main theses advanced in the book to show precisely how my understanding of groups will shed new light on some of the main controversies in social theory and applied ethics. In chapter one I ask the question: What kind of entity is a social group? I first consider the view that social groups do not exist, only individual human persons exist. This view is shown to be faulty because reference must be made to structures and relationships in addition to individual human persons for fully adequate explanations of such events as "Gulf Oil Company left Pittsburgh." Second, I consider the view that social groups exist in their own right, perhaps as full moral agents. This view is also rejected because it is shown that we do not need to reify social groups in order to make sense of the actual evidence of formally organized as well as informal groups. Finally, a middle position is developed in which social groups are conceived as individuals *in* relationships. It makes sense to refer to individuals in relationships, rather than to individuals conceived apart from their relationships, when there is action or intent that occurs in the group which could not occur outside of the group. In the subsequent two chapters an extensive argument is provided to show the wide range of cases in which this middle position is better able to account for the psychological and sociological evidence than can either individualism or collectivism.

In chapter two, I begin this argument with the difficult case of the purported action of a mob. I show that the mob is neither an entity in its own right nor an entity whose behavior can be understood as merely the aggregate actions of its members. Following suggestions made by Sartre, I show that the relationship of "solidarity" facilitates the joint action of the mob. I then extend the application of my middle position to formally organized groups such as corporations and informally organized groups, such as professional associations. In each case it is the structure of the group that facilitates joint action, action which is conceptually quite different from aggregated actions of individual human persons. I am most interested in such cases as the storming of the Bastille by the Paris mob in 1789, and the actions of employees under the supervision of managers of a corporation.

In chapter three, I take up the question of how collective intent should be conceptualized. I begin with a summary of the views of Jean-Paul Sartre on the subject of collective consciousness. I then present a number of sociological findings showing that corporations and mobs act in goal-directed ways even though the members of these groups are often not reflectively aware that their actions are so directed, and even though these members would not have engaged in such behavior on their own. I conclude that the full explanation of such goal-directed, purposive behavior must include some reference to the structure of the group. In addition, I argue that in the cases where such reference is necessary, it does make sense to talk about the collective intent of these groups.

In chapter four, I draw on the previous two chapters to argue that some organized and unorganized social groups can be held collectively responsible for the consequences resulting from their actions. When it is legitimate to attribute both action and intent to the members of the group, and when such action and intent is at least partially caused by the structure of the group, then such attributions of collective responsibility can be made. In the final two sections of this chapter I take up the question: How should responsibility be distributed when a group is held collectively responsible? I argue that, especially when the conduct of the group has been harmful (or criminal), key members of the group who played leadership roles within the group should be singled out as most deserving of blame (or punishment).

In chapter five, I address the question: Must a group undertake a genuine act, that is, must its members engage in jointly purposive behavior ascribable to the group, in order for it to be properly ascribed interests, harms, and rights? I argue that the capacity to act is not required as long as there is a sufficient interdependency of members, either in terms of the self-perceptions of the members of the group, or in terms of how these members are treated by others. In such cases, all of the members can be said to have the common interest that no individual or group adversely treat any member of the group indiscriminately. It is not necessary that the members of a group are aware that they have such interdependency, or that there are others engaged in indiscriminate treatment. Drawing on this analysis, I explicate the notions of common interest for the group of Blacks in South Africa, and for the members of corporations. I then begin to connect this discussion to the subject of group rights, that is, to claims made when the common interests of a group have been infringed.

In chapter six, I argue that the harmfully indiscriminate treatment of members of an interdependent social group can cause harm to the group. Each member is harmed either directly or vicariously whenever one member is harmed simply for being a member. I take up the case of negative stereotyping, a clear example of harms which are inflicted on members of social groups simply in virtue of their group membership. I argue that these harms are best conceived as group-based, and hence these harms can be the legitimate subject of group compensation programs. I then contrast negative stereotyping of unorganized groups with the denial of free speech rights to corporations. I argue that such corporate harm is not the kind of group-based harm that deserves group compensation. Group-based compensation is deserved only when the harms are likely to be distributed throughout the membership of a given social group. This condition is much more likely to be met for unorganized than for organized groups since the identifying characteristics of an unorganized group, such as Blacks, are the same as the characteristics which each member shares in common.

Finally, in chapter seven, I take up the subject of conflicts that arise between groups and individuals when political or legal strategies that are aimed at compensating groups for harm and denial of right, violate the rights of individuals. Justice is often said, most especially by libertarians, to be based on individual right. I argue that this is not a fair way to characterize the domain of justice. Justice must consider the number of people affected by a given policy, and must occasionally side with groups over individuals, even where rights are at stake. I conclude by applying this understanding to a particular case, namely, the Reagan administration's decision to disallow publicly funded lawyers from engaging in class action suits for groups of poor clients.

The greatest bulk of contemporary work on the ethics of groups has concerned the subjects of collective responsibility and distributive justice. Collective responsibility is generally treated as a deplorable ethical concept, a carry-over from our barbaric, tribal past. And distributive justice is seen as circumscribed by considerations of individual rights. In both cases, I find myself in severe disagreement with the dominant views espoused by my colleagues in applied ethics. In chapters four and seven respectively I defend conceptions of responsibility and justice as applied to groups which directly confront these reigning views.

1. The Nature of Social Groups

What kind of entity is a social group? Since the Middle Ages this question has been of central importance in metaphysics, but moral philosophers have not generally given it as much attention. My own view is that social groups should be analyzed as individuals *in relationships*. Groups themselves do not exist in their own right; but the individuals who compose groups also are often not understandable as acting in isolation from one another. Reducing groups to individuals *in relationships* achieves the task of demystifying our talk of groups as wholes in themselves, and also stresses that there is something social or group-based which remains important for the understanding of the actions and interests of groups.

Reification should be avoided in discussing and explaining the social world; but also our explanations and discussions need to be complete. If we can conceive of groups as involving no superentity but only the individual members of the group — if for example we can conceive of what a "corporation" does simply in terms of what its individual members do — then we should, all other things being equal, dispense with the additional baggage of group concepts and explanatory terms. Yet, at the same time, this reduction to individual terms and concepts should not be carried to the point at which one becomes unable to explain the social world. Such explanation often requires predicates which refer to social relationships. Concepts such as "being poor," "cashing a check," etc., require some reference to the interconnections among individuals, not just the individuals themselves. In this first chapter I will develop a middle position between those who wish to reduce groups to individuals and those who see groups as superpersonal entities.

My position will only be outlined in this first chapter; the argumentation in support of this position will largely be delayed until subsequent chapters where it will be shown that my position is better able to handle various cases than are competing views. The purpose of the first chapter, then, is to set out these competing views in some detail, and to contrast these views with my own position in the context of the contemporary philosophical literature about how to treat groups in moral theory.

In the first section of this chapter I will examine several theorists who argue *against* the existence of social groups by claiming that groups are nothing more than the individuals that constitute them. The first position, advanced by Lon Fuller is that social groups are fictions and that talk of groups cannot be justified by reference to the entities existing in the world. Since groups are fictions, then the structure of a social group is irrelevant in determining whether that collection of persons should be referred to as a unit. The second position I will consider is one which was prevalent in the 1950s among philosophers of social science. This view holds that methodologically one does not need social groups in order to render adequate explanations of social facts. All talk of social groups can be reduced to talk of individual persons. Such fictions are said to refer to institutional facts and anonymous individuals which are necessary in the explanations of group behavior employed by social scientists. I will be sharply critical of this approach.

In the second section of this chapter, I will examine several representative views that argue *for* the existence of social groups. The first view, taken by Durkheim, argues that there are social wholes which are entities in their own right, existing independently of the individual humans who compose those wholes. The second view, espoused by Peter French, argues that, methodologically speaking, one cannot fully explain certain kinds of group action without admitting that social groups such as corporations are agents in their own right. I will also offer criticisms of both of these views.

Finally, I will discuss two theorists who attempt to carve out a middle position on the nature of social groups by taking account of the structure of groups. I agree with each theorist that structure is metaphysically and ethically important. But each view fails to capture part of the range of activity of social groups in contemporary society and must therefore be rejected or amended. My own view is largely pragmatic: if a collection of persons displays the ability to engage in joint action or to have common interests, then this collection of persons should be conceived as a group. The two views closest to my own are not able to include certain groups which display joint action or common interest, and as a result these views are not wholly acceptable.

I. Against the Existence of Social Groups

Legal theorists have insisted for centuries that corporations, guilds, universities, and other social groups exist only as creations of the legal imagination. Lon Fuller begins his important book, *Legal Fictions*, by asserting: "Probably no lawyer would deny that judges and writers on legal topics frequently make statements they know to be false."[1] Contending that these quite common "conceits of the legal imagination" are fictions accepted by the legal community, Fuller argues that no one seriously believes that corporations have personality or that these groups of people are real in the way that human persons are real. Indeed, he says that the attribution of characteristics of individual human persons to a group such as a corporation is fictitious, that is, it is a literally false statement although one which is not intentionally deceptive.

For Fuller, social groups are fictions in that more is attributed to the group than is warranted by the properties of the group. For example, a corporation is said to be a person because its unity resembles the unity of an individual person. And while this attribution is thus based somewhat in facts about unity, an act of creative imagination is needed to conceptualize the corporation as having as much unity as an individual person has. Fuller says that:

> No one can deny that the group of persons forming a corporation is treated, legally and extralegally, as a "unit." "Unity" is always a matter of subjective convenience. I may treat all the hams hanging in a butcher shop as a "unit"—their "unity" consists in the fact that they are hanging in the same butcher shop. Certainly there is a more easily explained "unity" in a corporation than there is in such everyday concepts as "the 9:10 train for Chicago." It is also clear that the corporation, taken as a unit, must be treated by the courts and legislatures in that somewhat complex fashion which we epitomize by saying that legal rights and duties are attributed to the corporation. It is further clear that this treatment of the corporation bears a striking (though

not complete) resemblance to that accorded "natural persons." It then
follows that natural persons and corporations are to some extent treated
in the same way in the law; they form a "class."[2]

I agree completely with Fuller that what makes it reasonable to
call a group of persons "a corporation" is that this group displays a
certain kind of unity. Indeed, it is my position that the social group
has as its defining criterion a relationship among its members in which
a kind of unity results. Fuller is right to think that the "unity" attributed
to individual persons is not the same as that attributed to groups of
persons. Of course, human persons have parts, and in some sense
it is the finger that pulls the trigger, rather than the person. But the
finger is attached to the person, indeed this specific finger is an integral part of that person; whereas the specific members of corporations are not integral, they are each interchangable with other persons.

Fuller thinks that unity is ascribed solely as a matter of subjective convenience, but this analysis fails to distinguish types of unity.
People are able to discriminate between the unity of the hams in the
butcher shop and the unity of the members of a corporation. In the
former case, the hams share a common spatial location and are un-
doubtedly owned by the same person. But the fact that one ham is
spatially next to others does not affect the capabilities of that ham.
However, in the corporation the fact that one member stands in a
certain relationship to other members does make a difference in terms
of what that person can accomplish. And the fiction of attributing
unity to the corporation may very well be warranted in a nonsubjec-
tive way if this difference can be shown to be sufficiently significant.

Statements about the corporation are often statements not just
about the members of corporations, but also about the way these
members are related or unified. While it is a fiction to say that Gulf
Oil Company left Pittsburgh, since only humans can be properly said
to have acted, the statements made about the corporation are not
simply statements made about the corporation's members seen as
discrete human persons. Such statements also refer to an organizational structure whereby several persons, who are members of Gulf
Oil Company, are designated as those who will decide where all of
the members will work. The use of the fictitious phrase "Gulf Oil Company left Pittsburgh" can be justified by reference to the decision structure which related and partially transformed the actions of individual

board members and employees of this corporation. I will defend this point in detail in the second section of chapter two.

Fuller also claims that the chief test for whether a legal fiction is good or bad is that fiction's usefulness in a system of legal norms. If, for instance, it can be shown that treating the corporation as a unity or as a single person has good effects in certain circumstances, then the fiction can be justified; if in other circumstances there are no good effects from maintaining the fiction, then the fiction cannot be justified.[3] I think that this is a partially correct way to view fictions in both law and morality, but only if there is also sufficient evidence to link the fiction to structures and relationships that exist in the world. More is needed to justify the fictional use of a term than simply thinking that it serves a useful function, such as allowing a person to refer to a complex concept in a shorthand fashion. Convenience or utility is a major factor, but there must also be some metaphysical basis for these ascriptions. This does not mean that I favor the replacement of all fictional terms with factual terms.

Fuller recognized that there were problems with the use of fictions. He held that "we must not suppose that the 'thing' [the fiction] is something more than the sum-total of its properties."[4] The human mind naturally comes "to give too much credence to our analogies."[5] Fuller says that we tend to forget that the corporation is not exactly the same kind of person as is the human being. The corrective mechanism for this error involves "extracting from the word 'person' (when it applies to corporations) all those qualities and attributes not legally appropriate to the corporation."[6]

Perhaps the central philosophical problem with fictitious terms concerns whether there must be anything in nature to which these terms refer. When fictions are truly empty names, then the fiction does not refer to any existent entity, and many philosophers, myself included, want to avoid the quagmire of positing entities which do not exist. One interesting way of avoiding this difficulty is finding things in nature to which the fictional term refers. Rod Bertolet argues that when we utter "Pegasus is a winged horse," for example, what we do is refer not to something which does not exist, but instead to a Greek myth.[7] Thus, utterances "about Pegasus" can have meaning independently of the existential status of Pegasus itself. I will follow a strategy similar to Bertolet's in explaining legal fictions.

Since the only standard of evaluation with which Fuller leaves us is the purely pragmatic standard of whether the fiction is useful or not, his analysis is unable to say much about how to evaluate the truth or falsity of various claims made about legal fictions. Fuller regards these fictions as unconnected to the world, products of subjective convenience, not objective reality. Fuller is right to think that corporations themselves do not exist on some level different from those parts which constitute the corporation. However, those parts are not merely people but the structures and relationships among those people as well. The fictional use of the term "corporation" can be justified when the term refers to these structures and relationships.

The second view I will consider argues on methodological grounds that social groups need not exist. Known as "methodological individualism," the view developed to its fullest extent in the 1950s. One of its chief defenders, J. W. N. Watkins, offers the following definition of methodological individualism.

> Social processes and events should be explained by being deduced from (a) principles governing the behavior of participating individuals and (b) descriptions of their situations.[8]

What Watkins chiefly opposes is a view he calls methodological holism which explains social processes in terms of macroscopic laws and which posits the independent existence of social systems, which are seen as a type of organism or superentity. (The views of Durkheim, whom I consider in the next section, were thought to epitomize the holist's position.)

Watkins states the principle of methodological individualism first as an ontological and then as a methodological thesis.

> According to this principle, the ultimate constituents of the social world are individual people who act more or less appropriately in the light of their dispositions and understanding of their situation. Every complex social situation, institution, or event is the result of a particular configuration of individuals, their dispositions, situations, beliefs, and physical resources and environment. There may be unfinished or half-way explanations of large-scale social phenomena (say, full employment); but we shall not have arrived at rock-bottom explanations of such large-scale phenomena until we have deduced an account of them from statements about the dispositions, beliefs, resources, and inter-relations of individuals. (The individuals may remain anonymous and only typical dispositions, etc. may be attributed to them.)[9]

Watkins' defense of this principle amounts to an attempt to show that even the most complex social phenomena can be adequately explained by reference only to individuals. To provide these explanations Watkins posits several highly suspicious entities, as suggested in his final parenthetical remark in the above passage. Such devices as reducing all talk of social groups and institutions to talk of individuals are employed in an attempt to show the empirical adequacy of methodological individualism.

Watkins holds a number of assumptions which I regard as suspect. First, he contends that social explanations are best seen as reconstructions of what rational people would have done in given situations. This assumption unneccessarily obscures the phenomena under investigation. Second, in an attempt to completely reduce social phenomena to individualistic terms, Watkins posits a construction he calls "anonymous individuals" which is suspect on empirical grounds. More importantly, these entities, while individualistic in some sense, completely undermine any individualistic explanatory scheme. I will examine each of these points in detail.

Watkins and other methodological individualists rely on rational reconstructions to explain social phenomena. Watkins' view is clear from the following passage at the end of his essay on historical explanation.

> Society is a system of unobservable relationships between individuals whose interaction produces certain measurable sociological phenomena. We can apprehend an unobservable social system by reconstructing it theoretically from what is known of individual dispositions, beliefs and relationships. . . . Individualistic ideal types of explanatory power are constructed by first discerning the form of typical, socially significant, dispositions, and then by demonstrating how, in various typical situations, these lead to certain principles of behavior.[10]

While it is correct to say that social systems are unobservable, Watkins goes further in saying that "society is a system of unobservable relationships." A certain amount of reconstruction often has to be done in order to move from the indirect evidence of the relationships to their true character, but it goes beyond the evidence to say that all human behavior must be reconstructed so that the actions are portrayed as rational. Going beyond the evidence in this way, as I will argue, is a self-defeating strategy for methodological individualists.

The second point that social phenomena should be explained in terms of "anonymous individuals" is closely related to the point about rational reconstruction of the evidence. The "anonymous individuals" are the ideal types, or projections, that are based on what we know of human dispositions generally. They are characterized by the predictions we make based, for example, on projections about the behavior of average rational actors. "Anonymous individuals" are empirically grounded to a certain extent, since they are abstracted from the data of actual experience. But since they are so abstracted, they are also in another sense nonempirical. Any individualism that assigns an ontological status to "anonymous" or fictional individuals is an individualism which will undermine the ontological position methodological individualists sought to promote. In understanding the full implications of Watkins' suggestion here, some of the work of May Brodbeck, who criticized Watkins on this and other scores in the 1950s, is particularly helpful.

Brodbeck argues that Watkins' "anonymous individuals" either are a type of statistical concept, or else they refer to a list of behaviors which cannot yet be sharply defined. She argues that the statement "an increased dividend is anticipated" does not refer to a single individual, or even to several known individuals. Nonetheless, one could poll all of the individual shareholders to determine which ones did anticipate the dividend. The statement "an increased dividend is anticipated" is thus "a statistical concept, even though covertly in ordinary speech." While it is true that Watkins' claim that these statements do not refer to some superentity has some merit, he is wrong to think that these statements are about anonymous individuals. Brodbeck also argues that statements such as "the Jewish race is cohesive" do not refer to various behaviors "anonymously." Such statements have "open-endedness," but do not make reference to particular individuals. Specifically, "the Jewish race is cohesive" means "Jews usually marry Jews, live in close communities, share religious rituals, etc." Just because not all of the behaviors can be filled in at the moment, does not mean that they could not, in principle, be filled in.[11]

One of the unacknowledged results of Brodbeck's criticisms is that Watkins' reliance on concepts such as "anonymous individuals" actually undermines an individualistic approach to social groups. By failing to reduce the concept "anonymous individuals" to that of specific individuals, Watkins grants it the status of a separate ontological category from that of regular, observable individuals. He does this in an attempt to preserve the ability of his explanatory scheme reductively to explain such concepts as "society" solely in individual terms. But by admitting a nonempirical category into his ontology, the door is opened for other nonempirical entities such as the very social entities he is trying to eliminate. Indeed, anonymous individuals are no less theoretical constructions or abstractions than are holistic entities. It is difficult to discern a methodological rationale for ruling out only the former and not the latter.

Watkins extensively discusses those facts which do not seem to be about observable entities. In this class would fall facts about social groups. Groups are able to act and yet the process of behavior which generated the joint action of the group's members is often difficult to pick out. Watkins posits the existence of anonymous individuals rather than admit that statements about group action are about more than individual actions.

My proposal is to posit entities only when there are good *ontological* reasons for doing so. What needs explaining ontologically are the ways that individual persons are related to each other in groups and thereby enabled to act in ways they could not act otherwise. One does not need to bring in a whole different class of individuals to explain this enabling. The capacities of individuals change when they are mixed together with other individuals. This change is best captured, it seems to me, by reference to the structure of the group so formed rather than to an idealization of what would be occurring if each person were ideally rational.

We are now in a position to advance a preliminary judgment about methodological individualism. Methodological individualists admitted too much in trying to retain a strictly individualistic analysis of collective behavior. These theorists have posited fictional individual entities rather than admitting nonindividual entites into their ontological landscape. But if any entities are to be posited along with real individual persons, it seems that they should be the structures and relationships that exist among these real persons, rather than idealizations of these persons. Here the best evidence in support of my claim will be found in the analysis of cases begun in chapter two. Positing the existence of ontologically significant structures will be shown to be much more defensible than positing the existence of such creations as Watkins' "anonymous individuals."

II. For the Existence of Social Groups

At the end of the nineteenth century, a debate raged on a subject closely related to the one we have been examining: Whether there are facts which are irreducibly social and whether these social facts are such that the recognition of them causes us to change our ontological commitments. In this section I will first sketch the position of one of the chief defenders of the existence of social groups, Emile Durkheim. Second, I will sketch the views of Peter French who has attempted to refute methodological individualism in favor of a version of collectivism. Throughout this section I will try to show why a middle position between individualism and holism (or collectivism) is preferable to either alternative.

Emile Durkheim provides an exceptionally clear statement of a holistic account of social facts in his book *The Rules of Sociological Method* (1895).

> It is, however, the collective aspects of the beliefs, tendencies, and practices of a group that characterize truly social phenomena. . . . Indeed, certain of these social manners of acting and thinking acquire, by reason of their repetition, a certain rigidity which on its own account crystallizes them, so to speak, and isolates them from the particular events which reflect them. Thus, they acquire a body, a tangible form, and constitute a reality in their own right, quite distinct from the individual facts which produce it.[12]

Durkheim conceives a social fact to be a fact in its own right, quite distinct from the individual facts which have given rise to it. He admits that there must be individual facts which have caused the social fact to come into being, yet, there is a kind of transformation of the individual facts that then occurs. The chief evidence for this transformation and the disconnection of the social facts from the individual facts comes from the way that individual persons are influenced by such social forces as traditions and customs which form the basis of collective beliefs. Durkheim claims that individuals are greatly influenced by the collective beliefs of previous generations, as these are embodied (perhaps literally, as one can see from the quote above) in the laws and moral customs of given societies. It appears that individual persons cannot avoid being so influenced. In light of this, Durkheim argues that collective beliefs and traditions are independent of the conscious beliefs and wills of contemporary persons. The social influence is independent of individual influence.

Durkheim claims specifically that "when I fulfill my obligations as brother, husband or citizen, when I execute my contracts, I perform duties which are defined externally to myself and my acts, in law and in custom." These duties have an objective reality "for I did not create them; I merely inherited them through my education."[13] These ways of thinking and of acting are external, most importantly, to individual consciousness, for even when the individual is not aware of what his or her duties are, he or she remains bound by these forces. Durkheim thus argues forcefully that social forces exist which are independent of individual forces.

Durkheim uses the language of constraint and coercion to describe the influence of these social forces upon contemporary individuals. He claims that:

> From the very first hours of his life, we compel him to eat, to drink, and sleep at regular hours; we constrain him to cleanliness, calmness, and obedience; later we exert pressure upon him in order that he may learn proper consideration for others, respect for customs and conventions, the need for work, etc. If, in time, constraint ceases to be felt, it is because it gradually gives rise to habits and to internal tendencies that render constraint unnecessary. . . . This unremitting pressure to which the child is subjected is the very pressure of the social milieu which tends to fashion him into its own image, and of which the parents and teachers are merely the representatives and intermediaries.[14]

Since this influence starts at such an early stage in life, it is beyond the individual's control. And as the individual gets older, the traditions in which she or he was trained crystallize in such a way that she or he is motivated quite independently of the individuals who originally taught the person these traditions.

Societies are generated out of such collective beliefs and traditions which are passed on by individuals, but which are not themselves changeable by specific individuals. Other social groups, such as corporations and professional associations, come to have a life of their own as the collective beliefs and traditions of the group become deeply embedded in the psychologies of the individual members of the group. Durkheim claims that these groups are irreducibly social because the collective beliefs and traditions can exist even when they are not currently instantiated by individual persons.[15] In another of his works, Durkheim speaks of the division of labor as being one such example of a social fact which can exist independently of individual wills.[16] When collective beliefs become so deeply embedded that they are no longer under the control of individual wills, and when traditions can exist even when not instantiated in individuals, then social facts are best described as emanating from social groups. For these reasons, Durkheim claims that social groups are organic entities which can have a life of their own.

Durkheim is right to maintain that social traditions have an ontological status (a reality) which is different from that of individual persons. This is also true of social relationships. But he further contends that the social groups created by the combination of individuals and these traditions or relationships, through a process of crystallization, become components in a new reality — the social fact — which is "quite distinct from the individual facts which produce it." While Durkheim has established that there is more going on, ontologically, in groups than can be captured by examining the individual members of these groups, he has not provided the argument to show that there are facts or entities which have achieved an independent reality in their own right.

If Durkheim's thesis that social facts are about "the collective aspects of the beliefs, tendencies and practices of a group" means that our language of social groups refers to entities which are completely independent of the individuals who compose them, then his thesis is not compelling. A more plausible account is that social facts are best understood on the model of individuals in relationships. It is true that the relationships and traditions in a group can be characterized as the group's "collective aspect." But contrary to what Durkheim held, groups do not "acquire a body, a tangible form, and constitute a reality in their own right." It is not the group, properly speaking, which has independent ontological standing, independent of the members of the group in relationships.

Nonetheless, it is important that Durkheim was able to show that there are institutional and environmental factors which are essentially tied up with any social fact. Consider a case proposed by Maurice Mandelbaum in the 1950s, the example of "Jones cashing a check." It is quite difficult to explain this banking transaction merely by referring to the actions of Jones and the individual teller, since the very concept of banking relies on economic relationships which are not readily reducible to the interactions of isolated individual persons.[17] Durkheim believes that institutional and environmental factors constitute a social reality which is distinct from the individuals who participate in them. I believe that Durkheim's view goes too far beyond the evidence; however, one does need quite a subtle analysis of individuals in relationships to be able to account for such complex economic factors. I will attempt to provide such an analysis in the next two chapters.

In *Collective and Corporate Responsibility,*[18] Peter French tries to establish a nonindividualistic basis for understanding social groups. While his general approach is too restrictive, he does offer a useful typology of social groups, based on their structures, which I will follow in amended form.

French distinguishes between two types of social groups: aggregate collectivities and conglomerate collectivities.

> I shall call a group an 'aggregate collectivity' if it is merely a collection of people. A change in an aggregate's membership will always entail a change in the identity of the collection. In brief, a group or aggregate's existence as that particular aggregate is not compatible with a varying or frequently changing membership. The meaning of a sentence about an aggregate would be different if one of the individuals actually belonging to the aggregate had not, in fact, been a member of it.

> A conglomerate collectivity is an organization of individuals such that its identity is not exhausted by the conjunction of the identities of the persons in the organization. The existence of a conglomerate is compatible with a varying membership. A change in the specific persons associated in a conglomerate does not entail a corresponding change in the identity of the conglomerate. . . . what is predicable of a conglomerate is not necessarily predicable of all those or any of those individuals associated with it.[19]

French admits that aggregates can be easily handled by methodological individualists, since "what is predicable of an aggregate collectivity is reducible to the assignment of like predication (allowing for some verbal leeway) to collectivity members."[20] But, he holds that methodological individualism cannot explain conglomerate predication since this is not reducible to predication about individuals. French goes so far as to claim that a conglomerate is itself a type of individual which can be treated as a moral person in its own right.[21] While I think French's typology of social groups has merit, there are problems with his basis for distinguishing between the two types.

One of French's strongest arguments against a methodological individualist's understanding of conglomerate social groups concerns the individuation of these social groups.

> Suppose two lists have been compiled; Gulf Oil Corporation List A will be the list at 10:00 A.M. on Friday, October 7, 1983, and List B will be the list for 10:05 A.M. on the same day. The same names appear on both lists with one exception. On List A there appears the name "Bernard J. Ortcutt" followed by the job description 'clerk,' but that name is not found on List B. . . . Have we two different entities, (1) the Gulf Oil Corporation (List A) and (2) the Gulf Oil Corporation (List B), two different nonidentical corporations? I think not. And if this is correct, the existence of the corporate identity through time is rather indifferent to the shifting of the identities of those persons associated with it.[22]

Since the group cannot be reduced to a list of its individual members and their beliefs and behaviors, French claims to have found a good counterexample to the position advanced by Watkins and other methodological individualists. Unfortunately, French has overstated the case by saying that what is predicable of conglomerates need not be predicable of all or any of the members, as I will argue in the next chapter.

Most importantly, he is also wrong to think that aggregate behavior can be easily handled by methodological individualists. French admits that there are two subclasses of aggregates: "the sort whose definition explicitly involves spatial/temporal contiguity or . . . the sort defined in terms of a common characteristic or feature."[23] In the first subclass fall those random collectives which have no decision procedures and which are nothing more than the collection of people who happened to be in a certain place at a certain time. French's analysis is plausible for random aggregate groups. But the latter subclass of aggregates, those defined in terms of a common feature, is surely not one which can be understood as a summation of the parts of persons who compose it. Mobs and teams fall into the second subclass since both groups are defined by reference to the solidarity which allows the members of the group to engage in joint purposive behavior. A reductive analysis of the behavior of such groups would not be able to account for the collective actions or the common interests of which sociologists have found ample evidence.

Whether or not a group, and its behavior, can be reduced to its members, and their behavior, is determined by whether or not the structure of the group can facilitate joint action or common interest, and not, as French thinks, by whether or not there are fixed membership lists. Some groups have formal organizational structures, some have informal organizational structures, and some (such as mobs) can attain unity even though they are not organized at all. All three of these types of structure can facilitate joint action or common interest. Groups with these structures are to be distinguished from collections of persons which do not have the ability to engage in joint action. This latter group contains such examples as crowds and those random collections of individuals lined up at a bus stop. But teams and mobs can be shown to have sufficient structure to require a nonindividualistic analysis of their behaviors, even though they have no formal organizational structure. This will be the main thesis defended in the first section of chapter two.

The ontological status of the "relations" which turn individuals into groups should be carefully considered. Some theorists believe that these "relations" cause the groups to be real bearers of predicates, even though the "relations" themselves are not distinct ontological entities.[24] Other theorists hold that such relations are themselves "real," but what they relate is not the individual member to another member. Rather, each member is related to the whole, so that the group also must be posited as having reality in its own right.[25] My position is that "relations" among individuals do have a reality, a distinct ontological status which is different from the individuals who are so related. However, the reality of these relations is not sufficient to ensure that the groups, which are composed of individuals *in relationships*, have reality independently of the individuals who compose these groups.

Social relationships have reality in that they structure or unify a group of individual human persons so that these persons can act and have interests in different ways than they could on their own. In this sense social relationships have a reality which is distinct from individual human persons since the relationships are not themselves reducible to psychological, or other, features of individual human persons. An examination of the cases presented in the following chapters supports the conclusion that there is not, in addition, a separate reality for social groups. Individual persons and relationships have reality, but not social groups themselves.

Perhaps a brief example will help render this distinction plausible. Consider an amateur football team. The individual members of the team are able to run, block, and tackle on their own. But when they are joined together as a team each player is enabled to perform tasks that he or she could not perform merely as single individual ballplayers. The individuals are helped by one another, and because of this help each player is able to do more than he or she could do before. By the collective efforts of all the members, the capabilities of each member are enhanced. It is no longer possible to explain what occurs merely by referring to what each player does: some account must also be given of the cohesiveness of the group, of its division of labor, of its team spirit. These factors themselves have a reality which is not captured by describing what each of the players does. But the team itself does not have a separate reality from that of the members and their relations to each other.

The present chapter will end with a discussion of the structure of groups in light of two very recent essays in contemporary ethical theory. Through such discussion I will suggest what is wrong with more refined versions of individualism and holism (or collectivism) and expand my own view.

III. The Middle Position

So far I have provided reasons for rejecting two prominent answers to the question "Do social groups exist?" But, these answers were also found to contain much that was right. Certain legal theorists, such as Lon Fuller, are right to argue that to a certain extent talk of social groups is fictitious. And methodological individualists are right to argue that there is no good reason for positing the existence of social groups as superentities. But Durkheim and French maintain plausibly that an adequate explanation of the behavior of social groups cannot be given by reference only to the behaviors of discrete individual persons. In addition, the relationships and structures of these groups must be included in the explanation, and these components are essentially social in nature. In this final section, I will sketch a middle position, one in which it is possible to give both a qualified "yes" and a qualified "no" to the question: "Do social groups exist?"

Two recent essays, one by Richard De George and the other by David Copp, have tried to identify the ontologically unique basis of social groups by reference to the relationships and structures of those groups. These theorists have identified the traditions and documents, as well as the conscious beliefs and purposes, of the group members as that which allows us to see the unique structure of these groups.

Richard De George argues that radical individualism should be rejected because it cannot make sense of such things as natural human languages and cultures. Such things are not "the result of the activity of any given individual."[26] Also, radical collectivists are wrong to posit the existence of superentities since there is no such thing as a will or intention existing outside of individual persons. What gives reality to social groups, though, is the way in which individual persons are related to each other and to various institutions.

De George's view is quite close to my own, but differences emerge when De George holds that social relations manifest "the reality of a universal" when they are embodied in various documents. He sets out his position quite clearly when discussing the institution of marriage.

> Marriage, to take a specific example, is a social institution into which two people can enter . . . [yet] marriage is not merely a relation between two people, but a socially recognized relation with certain definite structures. Marriage, moreover, is a relation that is both a state and a process. . . . The relation of marriage as general is a social institution, a recognized form of relation for the people of a society. The form has the reality of a universal. The institution has embodied reality or matter in documents, laws, customs, and so on.[27]

Here De George suggests that it is the embodied matter of the documents, laws, and customs of a given institution that account for its reality as a universal. The social relation, as an institution, survives over time and informs the patterns of behavior engaged in by individuals.

De George puts his emphasis on how relations are embodied in the world, whereas I put the emphasis on how relations manifest themselves in the world by their effects. One implication of De George's view is that only those groups which are governed by "documents, laws, or customs" will count as having social reality as a group. He admits this when he says that because mobs lack any documents, laws, or customs, it is problematic to talk of these mobs as "acting."[28] This requirement unduly restricts the realm of social groups. As will emerge in the next chapter, mobs and amateur sports teams, for instance, can be seen as social groups, yet they are not embodied in the world in anything like the direct way that De George discusses. What makes me think that mobs and amateur sports teams should be seen as social groups, just as are corporations and nation states, is that their structures enable their members to perform actions they could not have performed on their own.

De George's interpretation is more appropriate in the case of institutional relations, which *formally* organized groups display. In the highly organized structures of corporations we come closest to that "embodied reality" which De George speaks of. The corporate charter and its often elaborate organizatonal chart, as well as the many internal procedures and rules, can be perceived directly as documents which embody corporate reality. Such reality is difficult to deny and even more difficult to make sense of merely by referring to the activities of discrete (perhaps even isolated) individuals.

De George has given us a criterion that allows us to distinguish types of social relationship by reference to these embodied documents, but he has not demonstrated why these documents and rules are necessary for the existence of social groups. If the members of a social group can take joint action or have common interests, why must they also be governed by explicit rules and customs in order to be properly considered a social group? De George is able to account for the actions and interests of unorganized groups only when there are background institutional rules and relationships already in place, as would be true in the case of a married couple or an amateur sports team. But in the case of mobs, there are no rules or customs of this sort. De George is left in the position of denying group status to mobs, even though they take actions and have interests. Yet having these characteristics indicates a kind of unity which would seemingly warrant the ascription of group status to mobs. De George admits that taking action and having interests are important for establishing the reality of nations and corporations, but he seemingly has no basis for denying the ascription of group status to mobs that also can act and have interests.

De George is correct to argue that in its characterization of social groups individualism fails to capture the importance of the relatedness of the individuals, especially in the case of individuals who comprise institutional organizations. Consider the modern corporation or professional association. In both instances there are individuals who act together (in some sense of the term) in such a way that it is common for group predicates to be used to describe their activities. Common usage presents at least a *prima facie* case for the appropriateness of such ascriptions.

The statement, "Gulf Oil Company left Pittsburgh," attributes a predicate "left Pittsburgh" to a collective term, "Gulf Oil Company," which stands for a group of individuals. Something important is lost when we merely describe what each of these individuals, *qua* individuals, did over the relevant period of time. Such a characterization fails to capture the way that these individual actions were facilitated through the organizational structure. If the structure of some non-organized groups can also facilitate joint action, then it would make sense to attribute group status to these groups also. But then De George cannot be right that formal organizational structures are necessary for the ascription of group status.

David Copp rejects Peter French's reliance on membership criteria as a way of distinguishing among types of groups. For Copp, an aggregate "is a complex of its stages," that is, a complex of persons or stages of persons' lives over a given period of time. Aggregates must have historical continuity of membership. Organizations, like aggregates, must have continuity of membership but also must have continuity of structure.[29] Copp says, "A mob may continue to besiege a city while various persons leave and others join it. Similarly, an audience may gain or lose members. Notice that we do not say that there is a new audience when a few latecomers arrive."[30]

Copp addresses the problem of group membership by saying that an aggregate (as well as an organization) is a "mereological" sum, not of its persons but of stages of persons. Copp explains the idea of a mereological sum, which he borrows from Nelson Goodman and Henry Leonard, as follows.

> The mereological sum of a set of entities is that entity which overlaps with every part of every entity in the set and with nothing else. It follows from this definition that a mereological sum is no less concrete than are the entities in the set which it sums. For instance, the mereological

sum of a set of gold bricks is itself a quantity of gold; perhaps it is a pile of gold bricks.[31]

Social groups are mereological sums of stages, or time slices, of the group, although each different type of social group may require a very different understanding of how these stages are united or summed.

Copp's mereological sum of stages of persons better captures the nature of aggregates than does French's membership criterion, which merely looks to the list or sum of persons who are current members. Copp's view is able to capture the fact that mobs, for instance, do change membership over time, but remain the same group. He is also correct to insist that this is because there remains continuity of membership, that is, most members stay the same over time, *and* there is a "unity relation," that is, something which is common to all members and which thereby links individual persons to one another. At the end of one of his papers, Copp likens a group to a deck of cards and a suit of clothes. Each part of the whole is an individual object. The parts stay the same over time and they have features in common which unify them a certain way. This account looks to the individuals and the relations among those individuals as the key components in a given group.

Copp thinks that the decision-making structure of a group is the most important unifying structure because this clearly allows for the attribution of choice to a group. But he does concede that even if a group lacked "an institutional decision procedure, we can attribute a choice to it if its members are unanimous in making this choice for the group."[32] There must be unanimity, Copp believes, because, like French and De George, he thinks that groups must have some mechanism by which individual intent is melded into group intent. An institutional decision procedure accomplishes this by imposing a rule on all members which makes the choices of some members count as the choices of each other member of the group. Unanimity of intent also assures that there has been a choice of purposes for the group which can be attributed to all of the members. With both of these mechanisms, it is now legitimate to say that every member of a group chooses the same purpose for the group, thereby creating a common purpose for these members.

Unfortunately, Copp has not fully appreciated the ways in which a common purpose may arise. His unanimity requirement makes it seem that there must be something like a vote that shows that each person has consciously chosen to agree with each other person in endorsing a given plan. And this implies that each person in the group is consciously aware that he or she has endorsed a given plan. It is my belief, which I will defend in chapter three, that a common purpose can be attributed to a group even if not all of the members are reflectively aware of having this purpose. In the case of mobs it is not at all clear that there is anything like a unanimous awareness of purpose for the mob members. Yet, without this condition, Copp cannot account for the actions of mobs. Nonetheless, the group's display of joint action, in such cases, is a legitimate basis for attributing common purpose to the group.

What is most attractive about Copp's view is that he posits a continuum, rather than a sharp demarcation, between organized and unorganized groups. A social group does not have to have a formal decision procedure in order to be assigned the status of moral agency. Indeed, as I will argue in chapters three and six, most of the members need not have any reflective understanding of being members of a group at all in order for the social group in question to be ascribed agency or harm predicates.

In summary then, it seems the fiction of a social group can be justifiably applied to those collections of persons which are interrelated in such ways as to be able to engage in joint action or to have common interests. Against French I argued that it need not be the case that all of the members of the group remain constant, nor that there be a decision procedure within the group, for it to be said that a social group is present. Against De George, I argued that it need not be the case that a social group have embodied reality through traditions, customs, or documents, and against Copp I argued that it need not be the case that the members be unanimous in their conscious goals, purposes, or desires. Each of these factors is important for understanding how certain types of social groups are able to act or to have interests, but there is at least one case where none of these factors is present and yet where a group can act — the case of mob action. The mob does display the feature I have identified as the chief characteristic of social groups: the mob can manifest itself in the world through the joint actions and common interests of its members.

The positive thesis of this chapter is that when a collection of persons displays either the capacity for joint action or common interest, then that collection of persons should be regarded as a group. The main argument in support of this thesis is that these capacities are what are commonly cited as the basis for the ascriptions of collective moral predicates to these persons. And while common usage does not settle all disputes in philosophy, it is certainly an indication of what is most intuitively plausible. The further plausibility of my thesis will only be seen in a careful examination of specific cases, where the intuitions underlying my thesis are tested. It is to these cases that I next turn.

2. Collective Action

In this chapter I will show how the previous understanding of the nature of social groups, developed in chapter one, can be applied to the concept of collective action. Three types of collective action will be examined: mob action, corporate action, and the action of informal associations. At the end I will set out my general strategy for analyzing collective actions. Throughout I will again defend a middle view on the status of collective predication: criticizing both individualist and collectivist ways of understanding why one is entitled to attribute an action to a group.

Are there any collective "actions" properly so-called? Methodological individualists deny that anything meaningful is expressed by the term "collective action." Collectivists, at least since Hegel, have endorsed the view that what actions there are, properly speaking, are the actions of groups such as nations and cultures. Surely, there is something to be said for both of these views, although there is much more wrong with them than is usually recognized. A consideration of cases will show that methodological individualists can explain the behavior of crowds but run into difficulty with mob action, and have great difficulty with organized action of the sort engaged in by corporations. On the other hand, collectivists have a relatively easy time characterizing highly organized activity, but great difficulty with the conduct of mobs. Both views also have difficulty with groups such as professional associations, which have only loose organizations but which are quite often said to act on their own.

My view is that actions are predicable of groups, even though the groups do not exist independently of the persons who are members of the group. As I said in the first chapter, statements can be legitimately made about fictional entities if there is something in the world to which the statements refer. In this present chapter, I will attempt to show that there is something existing in the world which warrants the predication of actions to the groups here considered: the mob, the corporation, and the professional association. In each case, it is the group's structure — how the members of the group are related to each other — that warrants the predication of action to these fictional entities.

No philosopher has been more concerned about collective action than Jean-Paul Sartre. Yet in contemporary debates on whether and to what extent groups can act, little attention has been paid to Sartre's work. This is partially due to the fact that Sartre was mainly interested in those cases of groups which were in transition from mere crowds to potent political forces in society, whereas contemporary debates have centered on the highly organized collective action found in corporations and nation states. For the two reigning schools of thought, individualism and collectivism, the paradigms of collective action have been the corporation and the random crowd. It has not been thought to be important to worry about actions in the middle of the spectrum as long as the ends of that spectrum have been properly conceptualized.

In contemporary moral theory and social philosophy, the prevailing wisdom is that it only makes sense to talk about collective action when the members of a group are linked by means of a strong organizational apparatus, and where the individual acts can be directed through some explicit decision-making structure.[1] The group action is then conceived on the model of individual action: a decision is reached, the organism sets its various parts in motion, and an action results. I will attempt to challenge this common model of understanding collective action by defending Sartre's claim that a mob can act, even though its members are not linked by any strong organizational apparatus, and even though it does not have an explicit decision-making structure.

Mobs are an especially interesting type of social group precisely because they themselves reside somewhere between the individualistic paradigm of random collections of individuals and the collectivist paradigm of the organic (or highly organized) group. On the subject of collective action, some individualists deny that there can be any truly collective action, whereas other individualists, such as J. W. N. Watkins, recognize only the type of collective action which seems to be based on some kind of common biological reaction by each and every member of a group.[2] Watkins claims, for instance, that when people are in a joint state of frenzy, in which each person is acting based solely on fear of a common enemy, then it may make sense to speak of a group acting, but only in such unusual cases.

Collectivists, as their name indicates, generally recognize the legitimacy of talk about collective action, but there is at least one important variety of collectivist, epitomized by Peter French, who does not recognize collective action unless it is the result of a highly structured decision procedure.[3] Informally structured groups are not said to be properly collective actors, and hence these groups are not held to be collectively responsible for the harms that they cause. Mob action provides a challenge to both of these dominant models since it is neither a special case in the way that frenzied behavior is nor the product of highly structured decision procedures.

There is one other important way of understanding collective action. Thomas Hobbes claimed that collective action can be conceived as representational (or what I call "vicarious") action. By this, Hobbes meant that collective action can be ascribed to a group of people if each member has agreed to let one or a subgroup of its members act in behalf of the whole group. This seems reasonable since basic actions can only be engaged in by individual persons, and so only through a relationship such as representation will it be possible for a group of persons to act. Hobbes admitted that there are various types of representational action other than the normal model of explicit representation found in political assemblies, but he never developed this suggestion.[4]

I. Mob Action

Sartre has claimed that what is needed for collective action to be ascribed to an unorganized group is some interest or outlook which each member of the group has in common with each other person. These interests and outlooks may link the people in such a way that they decide to follow a given member of the group in pursuing a strategy aimed at advancing their interests. Sartre, like Hobbes, is seeking a model of collective action which is tied to relationships among individuals rather than organization or decision making. I will begin by setting out some of Sartre's views on such cases as the Paris mob of 1789.[5]

Consider Sartre's description of the storming of the Bastille.

As early as 8 July (1789), Mirabeau had reported to the National Assembly (and his speech immediately became known to the Parisians) that 35,000 men were divided between Paris and Versailles, and that 20,000 more were expected. And Louis XVI answered the deputies thus: "I have to use my power to restore and maintain order in the capital. . . . These are my reasons for assembling troops around Paris." And on the morning of 12 July, the city was full of posters "by order of the king" announcing that the concentration of troops around Paris was intended to protect the city against bandits. . . . The rumors, the posters, the news (especially of Necker's departure) communicated their common designation to everyone. After 12 July 1789 the people of Paris were in a state of revolt. Their anger had deep causes, but as yet these had affected the people only in their common impotence. (Cold, hunger, etc., were all suffered either in resignation — serial behavior falsely presenting itself as individual virtue — or in unorganized outbursts, riots, etc.) This was followed by some incidents in Paris itself, at the barricades and the Tuileries Gardens, between military detachments and imitation gatherings (rassemblements d'imitation). These resulted in a new wave of serial defensive violence, and arsenals were looted. This revolutionary response to a constantly deteriorating situation has of course the historical significance of an organized common action. But this is just what it was not. It was a collective action: everyone was forced to arm himself by others' attempts to find arms, and everyone tried to get there before the Others because, in the context of this new scarcity, everyone's attempt to get a rifle became for the Others the risk of remaining unarmed. At the same time, this response was constituted by relations of imitation and contagion, everyone finding himself in the Other in the very way he followed in his footsteps. These violent, efficacious gatherings, however, were entirely inorganic. Here again, their unity was elsewhere, that is, it was both past and future. It was past in that the group had performed an action . . . it had been a group — and this group defined itself by a revolutionary action which made the process irreversible. And it was future in that the weapons themselves in so far as they had been taken for the sake of opposing concerted action by soldiers, suggested in their very materiality the possibility of concerted resistance. On this basis a dialectic established itself at the Hotel de Ville between the constituted authorities, which did not wish to hand out weapons, and which equivocated and found pretexts, and the crowd, which was increasingly threatening. . . . When rags were found in the boxes of arms promised by Flesselles the crowd felt that it had been tricked. . . . In tricking the crowd, Flesselles gave a sort of personal unity to the flight into alterity, and this personal unity was a necessary characteristic of the anger which expressed and, for the gathering, itself, revealed it. Everyone reacted in a new way: not as an individual, nor as an Other; but as an individual incarnation of the common person. . . . From this moment on, there is . . . the dissolution of the series into a fused group. And this group is . . . still unstructured.[6]

According to this description, the events in Paris in 1789 fused a merely serial ordering of random individual acts into an action which was collective in that the actions of each person were not done as the acts of an individual but as the acts of an "individual incarnation of the common person." Yet, the actions taken by the group at the Hotel de Ville and then at the Bastille itself were not structured; there was no formal organizational structure through which decisions were made by the members of this mob of Parisian citizens. Sartre follows in a long line of Marxist theorists who hold that collective action can occur when there has been a sufficiently strong common interest formed among individuals, and where these individuals find themselves identifying with each other in solidarity, rather than in their isolated individual identities. Sartre is quite clear in placing the "Other" in the role of catalyst in the formation of some groups. He argues that a group can come to have an identity through the way that collection of people is treated by other groups in a given society. The treatment at the hands of others, as in the case just described, causes the members of the crowd to see that they are already being treated by others as an undifferentiated, unified collective. According to Sartre, this self-consciousness, for each person, combines with the earlier realization that they have the ability to act as a group, and performs the task of "fusing" the members of the group into something like a common person, which acts in a concerted but unstructured way.

How can one tell when individual interest and consciousness are common among diverse persons, allowing for them to initiate a common intentional action in the world? Contractarian theorists, such as Thomas Hobbes, hold that a common will to act can be produced only by a common agreement and by a coercive influence to enforce the terms of the agreement. This agreement need not be anything which is explicit, or even which the individuals are consciously aware of. As a result, there do seem to be both Hobbesian elements in Sartre's example. The Paris mob, by the common reactions of each member to the injustices that had been perpetrated upon the lower classes, reached an implicit agreement to make demands in front of the Hotel de Ville and to storm the Bastille itself. And the coercive element came from outside, from the repressive actions taken by the soldiers and instigated by the Crown and the Assembly.

But what evidence is there for thinking that the Paris mob did take on a will of its own, in which each of the members of the mob had their wills subordinated to the common will? Since there was no decision-making structure, and since no votes were taken, it is quite difficult to show that each and every person in the mob had decided to subordinate his or her will to the larger will. And in any event, this so-called "common" or larger will can only be presumed to exist from the other facts that were observed, that is, the actions taken by the members of the group. It is the solidarity relationship between each member and each other member that indicates that there was more going on in Paris than the actions of single solitary individuals. And when these relationships of solidarity extend to all or most members of the group, then there is substance to Sartre's claim that there was a common will and something like a common person manifested by the actions of the members of the mob.

Methodological individualists and non-Marxist collectivists are in agreement in dismissing such examples as instances of merely aggregate action, rather than collective action properly so-called. Sartre's case is not dismissed so easily. Solidarity seems to be the kind of relationship which could turn a collection of individuals into a group which can act in a somewhat organized fashion, but this is not what Sartre claims. Instead, he holds that the Paris mob remained unorganized, even while it acted like a single person. For Sartre, the solidarity displayed by these people was not sufficient to bring them into an organized unity. Can it be that he thinks there is something which acts like a common person but does not display organized unity? In answering this question I will elaborate on Sartre's remarks concerning solidarity. But I will leave to the next chapter, on collective intent, the full analysis of solidarity as a basis of purposive behavior, restricting myself here to the way that solidarity functions as a unifying factor which enables joint action.

Solidarity is the key to the explanation of how a collection of individuals, such as the Paris mob, can be ascribed action predicates, such as "stormed the Bastille."[7] Crowds are not properly seen as the type of group that can act collectively simply because there are no relationships that exist between the members that would allow for such a characterization. The crowd is a grouping of random individuals, and the actions attributable to the group are ultimately reducible to the actions of the individual members. But the case which Sartre presents is quite different. The group at the Bastille or the Hotel de Ville in July of 1789 started out as a mere crowd or serial gathering. But various events, mainly events generated by the troops and the government officials who confronted the crowd, created within the members of the crowd a sense of purposiveness.

Solidarity turned the crowd in the Paris streets into a mob. It is the relationship of solidarity that makes the difference, and that makes it possible for the actions of these individuals to be treated as if they were the actions of a single entity. There was no real change in the number or type of entities in the Paris streets; rather, those who were in the streets became related to each other in solidarity and this made it possible for them to act in ways they previously could not (at least not under the label of a collective predicate). The Sartrean view has the advantage of providing a conceptual basis for understanding actions of the sort that methodological individualists cannot account for at all, and it does this without requiring that we multiply the number of entities in our social universe, as would be required in any collectivist account of these actions.

Mob action presents extreme difficulty for both individualist and collectivist accounts of group action. Individualists are left in the uncomfortable position of having to deny what is commonly recognized to be a fact, namely, that there was a collective action in the streets of Paris in 1789 which brought down the Bastille. Collectivists also have difficulty since the mob did not have an explicit decision-making structure or any of the other normally cited mechanisms of organization. The mob attained a status somewhere between a random collection of individuals and an organized group. Its in-between status brings about a reexamination of the features necessary for the ascription of action to a group, bringing out the importance of relationships, in particular, the relationship of solidarity.

Solidarity does not seem to be at all similar to the formal, explicit decision-making structures that exist within a corporation. And in this sense Sartre is right to think that the mob is not organized. But there is another sense in which individuals can be unified which does not require that there be a formal, explicit decision-making procedure: they can be unified by common interest to act together to achieve a common purpose. This kind of relationship is normally manifested by very small groups where there is such unanimity of purpose that the members of the group appear to act as if they were one person.

Think of the members of an amateur sports team or of a small jazz ensemble. Over time, there comes to exist such a strong rapport between the members of a jazz quartet, for example, that they are able to play together, to sound as if there was only one person playing. The common interest which each of the four musicians share is the key. Needless to say, there are also important dissimilarities between the jazz quartet and the Paris mob. The members of the jazz quartet have been together for a long time and they share a common set of skills and a musical education which brings them to an understanding of the same musical practice.

Nonetheless, in both cases (the jazz quartet and the mob), the activities of each of the members are brought together so that it appears that the members have fused together into a single individual. But, of course, what is true in the case of the musicians is also true in the case of the Paris mob. There has not really been such a change — for each member retains his or her identity and ability to act as an individual, and this can be ascertained rather easily by observing the behavior of these members taken out of the situation of close proximity to the other members. Even though the mob lacks the same factors which brought the jazz quartet together, there are other factors that bring about the solidarity that the members of the Paris mob experienced. "Alterity" and Flessell's trickery are the key factors which Sartre mentioned as responsible for the formation of group solidarity. These factors need to be examined in more detail before we address the difficult question of how such a large group could become unified without any explicit decision-making procedure.

For Sartre, "alterity" is "a relation of separation, opposed to reciprocity." In the case of the Paris mob, each person was separated from the other by a recognition that there were only a limited number of guns, and that when another person got a gun, then it would be harder to protect oneself from that other person, and also harder to get a gun for oneself. And yet at the same time, as Sartre points out in the case of the serial group waiting at the bus stop, each person finds a kind of commonality in the recognition that each person is replaceable by the other — if I don't get a seat on this bus, Jones will, and I'll get a seat on the next bus. One comes to the concept of replaceability from the recognition that each is merely an instance of the common characteristic "being a bus rider." But this alterity also leads to a kind of unification, insofar as having a common character-istic makes them all members of the same group. In some sense, the members of the jazz quartet also begin in "alterity" as they perceive themselves to exist as replaceable jazz quartet members, initially iso-lated from each other but eventually deriving their identities through reference to the other.

The recognition that each is replaceable is intensified when there is an Other, an enemy or oppressor, who treats each member of the mob as being indistinguishable from each other member. The aware-ness of the Other creates a common interest for each member of the group. It is an interest in the sense that each person comes to care about how each other member is treated, for since each is treated as indistinguishable from each other, how your neighbor is treated counts as a strong indication of how you will be treated, or would have been treated had you been there instead of your neighbor. This interest is common because it is true for each person who thinks about it, for it is not based on subjective but objective conditions — namely, how the other is reacting toward each member of the group, *qua* group member, not *qua* individual. In the first instance, there is a common interest in that each person should be interested in the indiscriminate way people who are members of one's own group are being adversely treated. The common interest is a function of the adversarial rela-tionship between the Other and all group members.

In a more important sense, the fact of one's common vulnerability to adverse treatment, at least for those who are aware of it, creates a common reaction against the adverse treatment. For example, Flessell's trickery "gave a sort of personal unity" as a group member to the members of the group, as Sartre says. Each came to understand that Flessell's act was directed at each group member indiscriminately, and each reacted initially with fear and then with anger at the way that Flessell, as the Other, was treating each one of them. Hence, the recognition of common interest and fear together produce the sense of solidarity. For each member of the group both sees the common plight and the need for concerted action against the Other. Solidarity is thus a way of being interested in what is happening to one's fellow group members, and from it springs the capacity to act as a group.

Two questions remain of central importance: First, why should one think that every member of the group actually recognizes a common interest? And secondly, if it is the case that each member personally has this recognition, why couldn't an individualist accept the characterization just advanced? As will be discussed in chapter three, Sartre holds that solidarity may remain at the pre-reflective level for some of the members of the group. It remains there for one to direct one's awareness toward, but it need not be fully reflective. Such a characterization is necessary for doing justice to two phenomena associated with mob action. Some of the members of the mob often feel "swept away" with their fellow members without realizing at the time why they were so strongly drawn to follow the directions of a temporary leader of the group. And also, not every member of the group can articulate the common interests that motivate them to oppose the Other and to seek out fellow group members for support. Nonetheless, careful probing brings out such common interests for those who participate in the mob action.

The characterization provided so far might seem to be compatible with individualistic analyses of collective action, but such is not the case. Solidarity is a relationship which exists among individuals, but it is not itself merely a function of the individual psychological states of the members of the group. The relationships themselves not only influence the psychological states of the members, but they facilitate the ability of these members to engage in joint action. It is not merely the case, as Watkins would have us believe, that each just happens to have similar thoughts. Nor is it like Watkins' isolated case of frenzy as a fear-induced simlarity of reaction. Rather, each chooses to act in solidarity with the others, and each thereby comes to do those things which facilitate the actions of fellow group members without the need for votes being taken or explicit directions given. This will be the central thesis defended in section one of chapter three.

A methodological individualist such as J. W. N. Watkins cannot account for the relationship of solidarity merely in individualistic terms and hence cannot do justice to the phenomenon of mob action.

A collectivist, such as Peter French, cannot account for truly joint actions that do not result from explicit decision-making procedures, and hence cannot do justice to the phenomenon of mob action. The importance of the relationship of solidarity, especially as it provides a kind of authorization of acts done in common for each of the members of the group, calls for a middle level of conceptual analysis of mob action, and calls into question the adequacy of the two reigning models of collective action. Sartre's conceptualization of mob action should become a major focus of attention for contemporary philosophers interested in exploring this new alternative model of collective action.

II. Corporations and Vicarious Agency

In this section I will expand the discussion of collective action begun above by turning to an analysis of the actions of a formally organized group of people. In the introduction I spoke about the 1978 lawsuit filed against Yale University, charging the university with the sexual harassment of one of its students. On first view the charge was a strange one. Even if corporations could be moral or legal agents, surely in this case the act in question was performed by only one person, a professor, and all other members of the corporation did nothing. There was no decision by the board of directors or stockholders of Yale University to harass the woman student in question. Indeed, there didn't even appear to be a series of actions which would resemble a collective conspiracy. So then, in what sense could Yale University, as a corporation, be responsible for the harassment of one of its students? In what follows I will attempt to set out the theoretical underpinnings of a theory of corporate agency that could be used to make sense of this charge.

An entity, such as a corporation, may be an agent in various ways, and it is a mistake to view corporations as agents in the standard senses of that term. Corporations should not be treated as full moral persons, nor should they be treated as machines having the ability merely to act (or react) automatically. Corporations can only act vicariously, that is, through other persons, and for this reason should be given a unique status as agents. The term "act vicariously" means that an action can be attributed to a corporation because of a formal relationship that exists between the corporation and the entity which caused the action. This relationship will be shown to be something like that which exists between a representative and his or her constituents, where the constituents can be said to act through their representative.

P. S. Atiyah has claimed that present English law does allow for corporations to be treated as having personally acted. In tort law, one of the leading cases is *Lennards's Carrying Company, Ltd.* v. *Asiatic Petroleum Company, Ltd.* (1915). In this case it was recognized that:

> There are some servants or agents of a corporation who can be treated as "the directing mind and will of the corporation, the very ego and centre of personality of the corporation," whose acts will be attributed to the corporation, not by way of vicarious liability, but on the footing that their acts are those of the corporation itself.[8]

Peter French has recently argued that corporations can be actors in precisely this sense, thus making corporations "full-fledged moral persons."[9] French tries to sustain this thesis by demonstrating that corporations have distinct personalities. The decision structure of the corporation "licenses the descriptive transformation of events seen under another aspect as the acts of biological persons (those who occupy various positions on an organizational chart) as corporate acts by exposing the corporate character of those events."[10]

Several of Alvin Goldman's contentions about agency illustrate why corporations do not have the full moral personality requisite to be seen as moral persons. Goldman draws an important distinction between causation involving objects or substances and causation involving events or states. He is willing to allow that collective entities can act as causal agents. "I contend that in the case of agents, as in the case of other objects, there is no incompatibility between saying that a certain agent was the (object) cause of a certain event and saying that an event or state involving the agent was the (event) cause of the same effect."[11] But most philosophers who, like French, claim that corporations are agents do so in the "object," not the "event" sense. They agree with Goldman that for objects to be agents they must have properties which incline us to attribute desires and beliefs to them. Indeed it is for this reason that they try to show that there are corporate intentions guiding the corporate action.

In the previous chapter I argued that the view that corporations are persons is a fiction. But such fictions may be warranted if there are things in the world to which the fictitious terms refer. In section two of chapter three, I will try to show in what sense the so-called corporate intentions have such a referent. Here in the present section I wish to dispute French's more general point by showing that corporate agency is properly "event" rather than "object" agency by arguing that the correlate of corporate personality is not a specific entity that acts, but a process through which actions occur.

French claims that the transformation of individual acts into corporate acts occurs in the corporate boardroom.[12] I agree that this is one of the locations of that which warrants any talk of corporate action. But I disagree that there is anything like a synthesis that occurs here which is productive of a new object agent. Rather, the decision structure, the organizational chart, and the job descriptions within the corporation, shape or channel the individual acts of members in various ways. And the individual acts are affected by these structural characteristics of the corporation, but not so that there is anything like a new object which can be said to be acting instead of the individual persons. The individuals remain the object agents, and the corporation only manifests event causation.

The most convincing reason for conceptualizing the change of individual actions as an instance of event agency is that further actions of these individual persons could constitute a change in corporate behavior or even in corporate structure. If a sufficient number of the individual members agree, then there is nothing the corporation can do to override their decision. Without the input of these individual persons, there would be nothing to be worked upon by the corporate structure. And the structure itself does not form a new actor, since the individuals retain the ability to change the course of the corporate character, if a sufficient number agree on the type of change that is needed. The vicarious agency of the corporation is a form of event rather than object agency.

It has also been contended that the actions of corporations are best described as automatic, machine-like responses to external stimuli. John Ladd suggested this line of argumentation in an essay on the morality of formal organizations. He held that formal organizations

> are differentiated and defined by reference to their aims or goals [and] . . . any considerations that are not related to the aims or goals of an organization are automatically excluded as irrelevant to the

> decision-making process. . . . Again, the point is a logical one, namely,
> only those actions that are related to the goal of the organization are
> to be attributed to the organization; those actions that are inconsis-
> tent with it are attributed to the individual officers as individuals.[13]

Ladd contends that the corporation, as a formal organization, is merely
an instrument of the individual persons who compose it. It is best
viewed as a machine which cannot properly be described as being
morally responsible for what it does.[14]

Ladd's analysis makes use of a definition which is consistent with
legal usage, although not, I will argue, with common usage. Ladd
claims that formal organizations such as corporations are defined
within quite narrow limits and their actions are completely distinguished from the actions of their members. In legal usage this is also
true. Black's Law Dictionary defines a corporation as an entity "which
is regarded in law as having a personality and an existence distinct
from that of its several members, and which is, by the same authority,
vested with the capacity . . . of acting as a unit or a single individual
in matters relating to the common purpose of the association."[15] Yet,
in common usage we talk about the excessive profits made by Mobil
Oil Co. or the benevolent actions of the Ford Foundation. In Ladd's
view these actions are improperly described as the actions of these
formal organizations because these actions lie outside the proper purposes of the organization. While we could, by stipulation confine talk
of corporations to a much narrower class of actions than is done in
ordinary discourse, I do not think that this would be a useful strategy.

Ladd's strategy is especially suspect when the actions attributed
to corporations do not resemble automatic behavior patterns in which
there is a corporate directive and an immediate employee response.
Automatic behavior is purely reactive, involving no significant addition from stimulus to response. Most importantly it would make no
sense to suggest that there could be a description of Gulf Oil Co. acting beyond its goals and purposes which could not be better described
as various individuals, who just happened to be members of this
organization, acting. Yet, some actions performed by individuals can
be better described (or redescribed) as actions of the corporation even
though the actions take place outside the stated goals of those organizations. And because of this, the actions cannot be described as merely
the responses of individuals to the stimuli of corporate directives.

It seems to me that it is impossible to describe accurately the acts that occur in the corporate setting merely by referring to acts of the individual members of the corporation, and not mentioning in the description a casual role of the structure of the corporation. More often than not, the acts must be described with reference to the corporation, since the acts here are different from the acts of the individual members, just as a whole is different from its parts. Even when the corporate entity acts through its chief executive officers, it is not merely the case that these officers acted in various ways, one writing a report, a group voting on that report and then delegating one other member to execute the decision. Such a description would fail to capture the fact that Gulf Oil Co. acted, with the various individual acts of the officers being mere parts of that corporate action.

Yet it should be clear that just as the forest is not itself a full-fledged biological entity, so the corporation is not a full-fledged person.[16] Gulf Oil Co. does act in some sense of that term, but its acts are vicarious ones, and its personhood is thus greatly restricted. But, corporate agency is not restricted to such an extent that moral appraisal of its action is ruled out. There are actions of the corporation which can be morally blameworthy even though the corporation's agency status is much more restricted than that of full-fledged moral agents. (The subject of blameworthiness will be considered in much greater length in chapter four.)

I will now explicate the notion of vicarious agency. In most cases, the individual persons who are members of the corporation are facilitated in their action by the power which the corporation has delegated to them. If the corporation cannot act on its own, it might be asked, where does this power come from and how is it delegated? The enabling and delegating acts are also performed by persons who are members of the corporation. Could these acts have taken place without the corporate structure which is the defining characteristic of the corporate entity? Perhaps some of them could have, but they would not be describable as acts of the whole group of members of the corporation (those who acted as well as those who did not). Instead, they would be described as acts of individual persons cooperating with each other in various ways. Without the "incorporating act," whereby the acts of different persons are linked together, certain acts could not be described as corporate acts.

"Incorporating acts" are acts which were taken by individual persons contemporaneous with the establishment of a corporation. The institution of the corporation allowed these individuals to designate the fictitious entity called the corporation as that entity which represents them collectively. Thus, the incorporating act is similar to the act of voting whereby individual constituents establish the office of congressperson through whose agency the constituents can act collectively. The original stockholders, for instance, incorporate themselves and can then act through the corporation. But the stockholders, unlike the voters, cannot truly act through the corporation without the corporation itself acting through others, its supervisors, employees, etc.

The board of directors, acting as agent for the current stockholders, acts through the corporation, and the corporation acts through its employees. The act of incorporation created the formal structure whereby these various relationships were henceforth perpetuated. The defining characteristic of the corporation, which allows one to say that it acts when others act for it, is set by the rules and procedures adopted and formally agreed to by the stockholders. These incorporating acts also establish the board of directors as those individuals whose collective decisions will be called the corporation's decisions. Before specifying these relationships in more detail, it should again be emphasized that the important point here is that the vicarious agency comes first and the descriptive change comes only after this. The collection of citizens can act as a group only vicariously; the person who holds the office of representative can be described as acting for the group because of the status of vicarious actor to which he or she has consented.

Within corporations two types of structural arrangement can be seen, together contributing to the vicarious agency that, in turn, constitutes corporate agency. First, the stockholders individually initiate a decision-making process which culminates in the formation of a corporate structure whereby the stockholders can be said to act through the corporation. Second, the corporation itself can only carry out the decisions of the board acting for the stockholders through its designated agents: managers, supervisors, employees, etc. The corporation is thus, in a sense, a place-holder, standing for the stockholders who collectively act through the supervisors and employees. Unlike the legislative representative, through whose agency the constituents act, the corporation must itself act through someone who has object-agency, since it can neither originate the incorporating process nor the process which results in action.

Corporate actions can properly be said to occur only where there is a causal nexus between stockholders or board members, on the one hand, and supervisors or employees, on the other hand. If the board members, for instance, have collectively decided to create a job with a certain description, then anyone hired for that job who acts in conformity with the job description and whose actions are most likely not countermanded by a higher employee, acts for the corporate board and hence, in some sense, for the corporation. If the employee acts outside his or her job description or in a way opposed to specific orders from higher employees, his or her actions are not the actions of the corporation, since the causal nexus has been broken. In that case, the employee is solely responsible for the consequences of his or her action.

The biggest problem for a theory of corporate responsibility or liability is to ascertain when an employee, supervisor, or manager, etc., is acting on his or her own and when he or she is acting for the corporation. Once an employee has been hired and given a wide job description, then actions performed according to that job description are corporate actions unless or until an appropriate party gives a countermanding order to that employee. But it seems difficult to understand in what sense the corporation is responsible for the harmful actions of its employees when there is no corporate policy or intent that those actions occur, as seems to be most often the case in employee wrongdoing. Yet, in such cases (as I will argue in chapter four), the corporation may be responsible and blameworthy because of the casual nexus that exists and because of its negligence.

Corporations can only act vicariously because they do not have object-agent status. But groups of individuals, such as the group of constituents who vote for a political representative, are different in that each of them is an object-agent, *and* the agent they act through is what Hobbes called an animate rather than an inanimate artificial person. Such a person has object-agent status and hence could properly act on his or her own and can also thereby properly represent the group directly. The political representative is thus quite different from the corporation or even from those who act in the name of the corporation. The corporation cannot either authorize or act, and this is why it is, in a sense, a place-holder for those who can do one or the other of these tasks. The political representative, unlike the corporation, acts directly in a vicarious way for his or her constituency.

But corporate and political actions are similar in that there must be some natural person or group of persons who are designated to act in behalf of the group or institution. And for this designation to occur there must be some process whereby the group of individuals or the institution is able to choose and authorize the person who is to act vicariously for them. Some set of rules and procedures for collective decision making is necessary for corporate action. In the final section of this chapter I will develop another sense in which a group can act collectively that does not require a specific and formally organized decision procedure. Individuals can come to have the status of apparent authority to act vicariously for a group, and when this occurs it may be proper to say that the group has acted through the actions of the apparently authorized person. It is to this complex notion of apparent authority and the actions of informally organized groups that I now turn.

III. Apparent Authority and Informal Associations

Formal decision-making structures allow a collection of individuals to authorize the actions of one or more persons as the vicarious action of the whole group. But there are also less structured ways by which vicarious action can be attributed to a group of persons. Throughout this section I will refer to cases of "apparent authority" following the tradition in legal theory of employing this same phrase to refer to authority that has not been earned through the normal process of explicit assent on the part of the individuals who compose a given group. "Apparent authority," as the name indicates, refers to a set of conditions whereby a public expectation is created that a given person is acting as the representative of a group, even though the members of the group have not authorized this individual to engage in an action for the group.

A case that well illustrates the vicarious action of an informal group, is *American Society of Mechanical Engineers* v. *Hydrolevel Corporation* (72 L Ed 2d 330).[17] For several decades McDonnell and Miller, Inc. was the leading manufacturer of low-water fuel cutoff components for heating boilers. These devices prevented the dry firing or even the explosion of a boiler whose water had dropped below a critical level. By the middle of the 1960s Hydrolevel Corporation had entered the market competing against McDonnell and Miller. Hydrolevel's new cutoff device had a time delay mechanism which allowed the boiler to continue to function for a brief period of time after its water had dropped below the critical level. This feature was meant to allow for the possibility of a temporary fluctuation in the water level, due to "surges and bubbles," which would not necessitate the cutoff of the boiler. This seemed to be a practical way to avert unnecessary stopping and restarting of boilers. By early 1971 Hydrolevel had begun to convince some of McDonnell and Miller's more important customers to switch to the time delay cutoff device. McDonnell and Miller responded to this challenge by trying to obtain a ruling from the American Society of Mechanical Engineers that Hydrolevel's product was unsafe, since it did not immediately shut down dangerously functioning boilers.

The man who played the chief role in initiating and sustaining the challenge to Hydrolevel's new product was John W. James, a McDonnell and Miller Vice-President. James was also vice-chairman of the subcommittee of the American Society of Mechanical Engineers (hereafter A.S.M.E.) which drafted and interpreted that part of the Boiler and Pressure Vessel Code governing low-water fuel cutoffs. The Supreme Court gave the following description of the strategy employed by James:

> James and other M & M officials met with T. R. Hardin, the chairman of the Section IV Subcommittee. The participants at the meeting planned a course of action. They decided to send a letter to A.S.M.E.'s Boiler and Pressure Vessel Committee asking whether a fuel cutoff with a time delay would satisfy the requirements of HG-605 of Section IV. James and Hardin, as vice-chairman and chairman respectively, of the relevant subcommittee, cooperated in drafting the letter, one they thought would elicit a negative response. (72 L Ed 2d 336)

This letter was signed by another of McDonnell and Miller's vice-presidents and, following standard procedures, the letter was referred directly back to Hardin, who was left in an unsupervised position to respond to this letter. "As a result, Hardin [who was employed by an insurance company with close ties to M & M], one of the very authors of the inquiry, prepared the response."

The response to the McDonnell and Miller letter misinterpreted the code to the detriment of Hydrolevel's product. "As anticipated, M & M seized upon this interpretation of Section IV to discourage customers from buying Hydrolevel's product." When Hydrolevel learned of this, its president appealed the ruling, but by the time the appeal was heard John James was the chairman of the subcommittee. He recommended that A.S.M.E. confirm the intent of the original letter of response. Several years later, due to ever declining sales, Hydrolevel brought suit against A.S.M.E. and the companies that employed James and Hardin. "Prior to trial, Hydrolevel sold all its assets, except this suit, for salvage value" (72 L Ed 2d 338). James' and Hardin's companies settled out of court with Hydrolevel.

Hydrolevel charged that James and Hardin acted within the scope of their apparent authority as representatives (the legal term is "agent") of A.S.M.E. and thus A.S.M.E. itself could be held legally responsible for conspiring to act in restraint of trade, and hence in violation of the Sherman Antitrust Act. A.S.M.E., in its defense, claimed that it should only be held liable if it ratified the actions of James and Hardin, or if James and Hardin had acted in pursuit of A.S.M.E.'s interests. The majority of the United States Supreme Court sided with Hydrolevel.

It is often claimed (and was claimed in the Supreme Court's dissenting opinion in *A.S.M.E.* v. *Hydrolevel Corporation*) that professional associations are not formal organizations and are not capable of controlling the conduct of their various members. Since these associations can rarely enable or curtail the activities of their members, the actions of one member should not be identified as the actions of the profession. Unlike profit-making formal organizations, associations cannot threaten their members with loss of job or decrease in salary, thus effectively rendering the association powerless to control the conduct of its members. Associations are not in the business of group coordination, and, so it was claimed, their responsibilities and liabilities should reflect this status.

This common claim is wrongheaded for several reasons. First, the contention that associations are powerless to control the actions of their members is doubtful. Unlike random collections of individuals (such as those individuals who happened to be neighbors of Kitty Genovese) associations have decision-making mechanisms, or at least could develop them.[18] They are sufficiently structured to appoint agents to act in the association's behalf. In addition, these associations have at least the informal ability to censure members by publicly disassociating the professional group from the member in question. Since the members all seek the benefits of identification with the professional association, censure and disassociation could be serious clubs that the professional association may threaten to use against its members. It is true that a disassociated member can still (wrongly) claim to be a member of a professional association, yet such a person would nonetheless be seriously disadvantaged in other ways. For example, the disassociated member would lose access to the information disseminated by the association and the esteem of being an association member. Furthermore, when the association grants a member an influential position within the group, this often enables the member to act in ways he or she could not have acted before (at least not under the same description). Another club wielded by the association is retraction of an influential position within the association which would have the effect of disabling the member from engaging in certain types of actions.

Second, while it is not true that associations act every time one of their members acts, it is true that the association cannot act without doing so through one of its members. If the association can ever be properly said to act, it must do so vicariously through its members. And when it is said to act vicariously through its members, this is quite different from these members acting on their own. "Acting vicariously" means that one person acts in behalf of another, or conversely an entity acts through a person whose action is then redescribed as the action of the entity. The redescription which links the acts of the one individual with the group changes the character of the original action itself.

Engineering associations do perform tasks which greatly affect the way the public comes to regard the activities of its members, especially in those associations which have publicly proclaimed that their members are capable of rendering objective judgments on such questions as whether a certain product is safe or not. In *A.S.M.E.* v. *Hydrolevel Corporation* it was shown that the engineering association sought to promote its image as a determiner of whether new products met certain minimum safety standards. Because of its public proclamations about those who are its agents, the court ruled that A.S.M.E. should be held liable for the actions of its members who acted "within the scope of their apparent authority" even if these members intentionally misrepresented themselves in this respect. What is important, the Court of Appeals had declared, is that the public has been led reasonably to expect that certain members of an association are speaking in behalf of the association. It is difficult, if not impossible, for the members of the public to know for sure whether a supposed spokesperson or agent of the association is acting fraudulently. And there is the possibility of conflicts of interest developing due to the fact that members of these associations are also privately employed. As a result, the majority opinion of the Supreme Court agreed with the Court of Appeals that the association should be assigned the duty of minimizing possible abuse of the authority vested in its members. Thus, it becomes A.S.M.E.'s responsibility to guarantee that its self-created public expectations are realized, and to be responsible for the actions of its members who act under the apparent authority of the association. In what follows I will present several other arguments designed to add further support for this conclusion.

Some have contended that the apparent authority theory is not a theory of agency at all since it does not postulate the necessary conditions for the establishment of a real relation between principal and agent. Because apparent authority assigns agency without having to prove a causal connection between principal and agent, the Supreme Court's dissenting justices claimed that apparent authority might degenerate into a form of strict liability. To establish apparent authority it is not necessary that a principal actually delegate a certain function to an agent (the chief means of establishing real authority), but only that the third party believe that this delegation has occurred. These dissenting justices felt that there were many cases that would prove problematic if apparent authority was accepted. For example, if one has been told by countless radio announcers that the current president, Ronald Reagan, is the spokesperson for America, one may come to believe, and even be somewhat justified in believing, that when Reagan speaks America speaks through him. But this is quite a faulty way of establishing whether Reagan is or even should be seen as the spokesperson for America, and of whether America should be responsible for what Reagan says or does.

Before trying to counter this objection to the apparent authority theory, I must point out that there is a more defensible way of viewing the apparent authority theory than what was characterized above. What is important to this theory, for example, is not just that one believes, even reasonably, that Reagan is the spokesperson for America, but that one believes so because those for whom he is said to speak have generally authorized him to so speak and have not given any clear basis for deciding when he is not authorized to do so. Thus, apparent authority, in its more plausible form, requires not merely 1) that a person believe that x is the agent of y, and 2) that it is reasonable for that person to hold this belief, but also 3) that y has supplied these reasons, and has supplied no basis, which is accessible to that person, for defeating these reasons in a particular case. While the Court of Appeals mentioned this last requirement in passing, it was not singled out as the most important condition, yet surely it should have been.

If I initially delegate you to act for me and then fail to provide a way to show when you do not act for me, I have created a *prima facie* presumption that you are my representative. I must publicly announce that you are not my representative for this presumption to be rebutted. Private pronouncements on the subject are irrelevant. You remain my representative in all cases until I publicly disassociate myself from you. Apparent authority, on this more plausible reading of the theory, is not sufficiently distant from "real" authority to warrant the claim that it is not a theory of agency, or that it collapses into strict liability.

It seems to me that every principal-agent relationship is predominantly a function of what public appearance has been created by the acts of a principal toward the supposed agent of that principal. Three hundred years ago Thomas Hobbes made much the same point when talking of the act of delegation that creates the authority of a political ruler. Hobbes said that the delegation involves the signification (literally, the making of a public sign) of the actions of one person to be also another person's actions.[19] Since the character of these actions does not really change, that is, since the change is in name only, what is crucial is that others be made aware of this change publicly. Following Hobbes, I contend that it is a necessary feature of the principle-agent relationship that the principal indicate to others that the actions of some other person are to have a special signification, namely, that they are also to be understood to be (or are to be seen as if they were) the actions of the principal. And it is the members of the public who must be able to understand this fact. If this is indeed the correct account of the general nature of principal-agent relationships, then the apparent authority theory is no less a theory of agency for its heavy reliance on what the members of the public can reasonably be expected to believe. Thus, the Supreme Court's majority ruling that professional associations can be linked to their members as agents by the apparent authority theory is not as implausible as it first appeared.

How would the other theories of collective agency treat the *Hydrolevel* case? Individualist theories stress that there are really only particular persons acting in the world, and that talk of any other kind of superentity or organization acting is merely reification, reification that is ultimately pernicious. These thinkers would be suspicious of the claim that the principal-agent relationship is a matter of public appearances, and even more suspicious of the claim that one can attribute actions to a group that are based merely on these perceptions. This sounds too much like those who say that corporations and nation states act in the same way that human individuals act. To make the authority relationship a matter of appearances, and then to make the attribution of agency depend on the thin basis provided by these appearances, is to invite not only reification but also deception. We are much better off, they would argue, to stick to what can be clearly perceived, and that includes only the actions of individual persons.

While I agree with the empiricist sentiments expressed by most individualists, they err in assuming that there is a significant difference between what is the case and what appears to be the case, a difference which can be ascertained empirically. Yet, the way in which facts are ascertained empirically is precisely through the perceptions which each of us has, that is, through the way the world appears to each of us. If relationships are to be part of our ontological landscape (a matter which some individualists would deny to begin with) then there is no other basis for testing our initial impressions than the appearances. For relationships, such as that between principal and agent, are not particulars in the same way that persons are. Those who stand on the outside observing two people in a relationship cannot normally get independent confirmation of the existence of the relationships other than what the parties report and how these parties behave toward each other. It is for this reason that the concept of apparent authority is not necessarily at odds with empiricism.

But the caution expressed by individualists must be taken quite seriously. There must be a link established between the perceptions or expectations of the public and the actual behavior of the members of a group. This link will often be hard to establish, and as in the case of *A.S.M.E.* v. *Hydrolevel Corporation*, there will be many close calls. If the effect of this court ruling is to make judges less vigilant in attempting to identify the causes of the public perceptions of apparent authority, then there will indeed be a legitimate reason for the individualists to worry. But to reject apparent authority is to be unable to account for the quite commonsensical attribution of agency in the *Hydrolevel* case. We are left with either remaining cautious to the point of being counterintuitive, or of serving these intuitions and risking some mistakes in assessing collective action by adopting the theory of apparent authority. For the reasons I set out above, I favor the latter approach, although I recognize that this is an imperfect solution.

In a preliminary way, then, we can formulate the conditions which need to be satisfied in order for a group of persons to be legitimately ascribed actions.

1) individuals are related to each other so as to enable each other to act in ways they could not act on their own;

and 2) some individuals are authorized, or appear to be authorized, to represent their own actions as the actions of the group as a whole.

To meet this second condition it is not sufficient that some people merely believe that a given person, Jones, is the legitimate agent of a given group. Rather, this perception or expectation must be based both on the behavior of the apparent representative and on the behavior of the members of the group toward that apparent representative.

Collectivists would have the most trouble with the first of these two conditions for the attribution of agency. It might appear that the above account regards the normal situation from which collective action diverges as that of individual isolated action. Yet, such a suggestion would be described as misleading and pernicious by collectivists, such as Rom Harré. In his book *Social Being*, Harré contends that men "would not be men at all unless they were creations of the collectives in which they live."[20] Social action is something which is essential to the functioning of any person as a person, in Harré's estimation, and thus humans are enabled to act (as humans) in each instance by the social milieu of which they are inextricably a part. What arguments can be brought to confront this claim that all human action, not just collective action, is made possible by social relationships?

Perhaps the best way of disputing this charge by the collectivists is to point out that it is quite common to describe some human acts by reference to the causal history of one solitary human being. In addition, there are some, but only some, human actions which are commonly redescribed as the actions of a group of persons and hence as collective actions. Surely there is something important to be learned from these common uses of the terms "individual" and "collective" action. Harré and other collectivists do not seem to take seriously the fact that our common ways of describing the world involve a differentiation between collective and individual actions. I thus do not follow these collectivists in thinking that all human action is, at the time of the action, enabled by social factors, and I continue to support the first condition of collective action mentioned above.

Consider the problems posed by the actions ascribed to the Paris mob on the 14th of July in 1789. Cast in light of the previous discussion, the question is: When were the members of the Paris mob enabled to act, in ways they couldn't before, by the help they received from their fellow group members? And furthermore, when is it possible for outsiders to attribute "group action" to the actions of a representative mob member? As Sartre maintained, initially the Paris mob was not a group which could act, for individuals were merely in serial ordering, much like the people waiting in line for the bus. This random grouping of individuals did not act as a group; rather, they were merely individuals acting in close proximity to one another.

The actions of Flessell and the army produced a common objective for the individuals in the streets of Paris, and helped form solidarity among them. They were thereby enabled to act together toward a common objective. And then outsiders could be led to expect that any member did act for the group when that member acted in pursuit of that common objective. At a crucial stage the Paris mob ceased to be merely a random collection of individuals and became unified, and this change opened the door for the ascription of collective action.

I suggested at the end of the first section of this present chapter that solidarity is created out of a common interest of the mob members, and that this solidarity provides a kind of authorization of joint acts done in the common interest. Obviously, such authorization will be even more difficult to grasp than the apparent authority in the case of the professional association's actions. The authority in the mob, if indeed it can be so-called, comes from the sentiments of the members of the group, not necessarily from what the public is able to perceive, although there must be some observable cohesiveness to the mob for it to make sense to say that the "mob" has indeed acted. Such cases stretch the meaning and usefulness of the authority requirement in the above preliminary set of conditions for collective action.[21] This is because in mob action, unlike the other types of collective action considered in this chapter, the members do not participate by actually voting for representatives. Rather, if mob members engage in authorization at all they do so when they each "vote" by their actions. And if it is true that they need not be consciously aware of the fact that they have interests in common with other members of the group (as will be shown in the next chapter), then they also might not be consciously aware that their actions do indeed cast "votes" in favor of the joint undertaking.

I conclude therefore that the second condition mentioned above (the authorization condition) is essential only when not all members of a given group continue actively to participate in the joint undertakings of that group. Hence, the first condition (the enabling condition) is the only condition which is necessary across all forms of collective action. I will return to these considerations in chapter four, but now I must no longer delay considering the very difficult question of collective intent, especially as it functions in mobs. Only after this subject has been addressed can the investigation of specific moral categories, such as blameworthiness for action, proceed.

3. Collective Intent

When considering the moral status of groups, it is often claimed that since groups do not think or intend to act they cannot be conceived as moral agents. Two strategies have been proposed concerning putative cases of collective intent. Some philosophers have denied that there is anything more than individual thinking and intending organized in such a way that it appears to be the thinking and intending of the group. This strategy generally only allows talk of collective intent, if at all, in highly formal organizations. According to the second strategy, there is a genuine kind of collective intent but only where individuals reach a unanimity of judgment on the basis of a common interest shared by all group members and a common desire to succeed in a particular project oriented toward the common interest. The second strategy generally is thought to apply only to groups in which explicit votes have been taken. In this chapter I wish to assess these two explanatory strategies in light of a wider range of cases of group action than is normally undertaken. Throughout this chapter I will make extensive reference to what some major social theorists and sociologists have said about collective consciousness, solidarity, and corporate decision making.

In the first section of this chapter I will argue that the consciousness attributable to mobs does not fit well into either of these theoretical models. I will again turn to Jean-Paul Sartre, who made the only sustained attempt to capture the experience of collective consciousness in mobs. In the second section, I take up a very different case of collective intent — the decisions and plans reached in the corporate boardroom.

I. The Intentions of Mobs

Mobs do not have decision procedures which warrant the ascription of intentional states to these groups, and they also do not even have the kind of structure that allows for explicit voting about alternative courses of conduct to be pursued. Moreover, mobs are generally neither long-lasting nor hierarchically structured. Yet sociological and historical evidence suggests that some mobs have engaged in conduct that appears to be purposive and which even involves quite complex divisions of labor.

Consider the case which Sartre analyzes, the storming of the Bastille. Engravings made at the time show bands of Parisians engaging in quite complex behavior, such as removing very large stones from the walls of the Bastille. This type of action would normally be successful only if the people involved were organized and receiving explicit instructions from, for instance, a foreman. In addition, there are written and pictorial accounts of bands of the mob which broke off from the main group in order to perform specific tasks needed to be done at the moment, such as preventing a fire from going out or setting up barricades to keep out newly arriving soldiers. Again, this is the kind of activity which would normally succeed only if there were some central authority making decisions and issuing commands. Finally, the various activities of the mob lasted over three days, resulting ultimately in the destruction of a fortress which had previously resisted attack by well-organized groups of soldiers.[1]

This example illustrates several important features of mob action. First, it appears that mobs can engage in joint action directed toward specific goals even though there is no decision-making structure for the group. Second, the actions of each member of a mob can seemingly be related to the actions of other members, even though there is rarely any organizational structure to the mob. Third, the members of the mob seek to aid one another's efforts, in quite complex ways, even though there is no authority in the mob which directs the activities of these members. And finally, the actions need not be merely momentary, but can last for several days. For these reasons, I will follow Sartre in arguing that mobs can display a kind of collective intention in such cases as the storming of the Bastille.

In his discussion of collective political action in *The Critique of Dialectical Reason*, Sartre claims that there is a type of collective consciousness that can unify the members of an unorganized group such as a mob. Collective consciousness, on Sartre's view, is not necessarily something that the members of a group are fully aware of, but it does, nonetheless, motivate them to act in a concerted fashion and to sustain this social action sometimes over a substantial period of time. As we saw in the last chapter, Sartre's paradigm example here is the politically inspired mob, such as the group of Parisians who stormed the Bastille in 1789. This case of mob action is an interesting illustration of collective consciousness and intention by unorganized social groups, though by no means the only sort.

The most interesting aspect of Sartre's example is that some members of the mob did not act out of a fully reflective consciousness. In his earlier works, Sartre referred to this as pre-reflective or unreflective consciousness, that is, as a consciousness which is not reflected upon by the agent, and hence not something of which that agent is self-conscious. In attempting to analyze the pre-reflective consciousness which arises in certain tightly knit but unorganized groups, Sartre describes the experience of being part of the group.

> This group is not an object in any way and, in fact, *I never see it*; I totalize it *in so far as it sees me*, in so far as its praxis takes me as a means or an end. . . . In simple terms of perception, I can *see* the flight *of the group*, which is *my* flight, because, in the dialectical development of my *praxis*, I unite and coordinate similar or reciprocal actions (people *helping* one another to flee or to defend themselves). There is, therefore, something resembling one object fleeing on these hundred pair of legs.[2]

According to Sartre, the members of a mob can become conscious of the needs of the group and are hence conscious of what tasks need to be performed for sustaining the efforts of the group. However, the individuals in these groups are not necessarily reflectively aware of such consciousness. Again using a perceptual analogy, Sartre asserts that no member of large mobs can see all the other members, and yet each one may come to an awareness of the needs of the members of the mob.

The members of a mob can attain the kind of collective consciousness of each others' needs that unites them as if they were one organic totality. But in reality, as Sartre tries to show, the kind of synthesis necessary for a true melding of these individuals into an organic whole is impossible. The unity which is achieved in the mob falls short of what Sartre calls true totality, and yet he claims this unity is real, as seen by the fact that the mob members are motivated to act by the structure of the group.[3]

To explain the motivation of the mob members, Sartre contends that they manifest a "quasi-intentional" consciousness.[4] It is only quasi-intentional, in such cases as the storming of the Bastille, because the members did not necessarily come into the street in order to carry out some definite task, but in order to find others who shared their attitudes toward the king. When they approached the street, the objective of each of these persons, in terms of specific action to be taken against the king, was, in Sartre's words, "indeterminate."[5] After each person was in the street and had found others who were already engaged in action, they each followed along. At the reflective level, the intention might have been to aid their comrades in the street, but at the pre-reflective level, on Sartre's view, there was also an intention to storm the Bastille.

In his earlier work on philosophical psychology, Sartre foreshadows his discussion of quasi-intentional behavior of the members of the Paris mob. He tries to show, in those early writings, how pre-reflective consciousness could be purposive, in the sense of being problem-solving. In his book, *The Emotions: Outline of a Theory*, Sartre analyzes the change of approach that occurs when a person is suddenly able to solve a puzzle that has previously stymied him or her. Sartre says that the "impossibility of finding a solution" in our reflective consciousness sometimes serves as motivation for the pre-reflective consciousness "which now perceives the world otherwise and with a new aspect, and which requires a new behavior."[6] This state of pre-reflective consciousness can be a state which motivates the individual in a way similar to the motivation accruing from one's reflective awareness. Psychological research has confirmed Sartre's view. In a 1985 article, Virginia Blankenship, summarizing recent empirical work in this area, says that a narrow focus on actions that are fully under the conscious control of the agent ignores other important motivations, such as unconscious motivations, that are part of the multilayered nature of intentionality.[7]

Pre-reflective intentions are intentions which are not yet fixed as "my intentions" but which motivate me toward purposive action, for instance, within an unorganized group such as a mob. These pre-reflective intentions seem to arise out of the collective relations of a group such as a mob, specifically out of solidarity. If such intentions arise out of what is collective, not what is individual, then we can begin to explain how people could be motivated to act in purposive

ways without having reflected upon what they are thinking and doing. If Sartre is right to say that pre-reflective consciousness does not
need reflection to make it a real motivator of human persons,[8] then
it might make sense to say that these mob members have pre-reflective
intentions which are motivating their actions.

As far as I know Sartre never explicitly linked pre-reflective consciousness to the concept of intent. This linkage is my own. Partially
following Sartre, then, it seems plausible to think that there can be
pre-reflective intentions, that is, intentions which are not yet reflected
upon by each of the members of an unorganized group. And sociological evidence supports this account.

The notion of solidarity is the key to understanding how people
can be collectively motivated to engage in purposive action even though
the group is not organized. Sociologists have written about solidarity
for almost as long as there has been sociology. Emile Durkheim defines
solidarity to be the set of sentiments a person has toward other persons of one's group, in which the interests of the members of that group
are made the interests of the individual in question. Max Weber
similarly defines communal solidarity in social relationships in terms
of "a subjective feeling of the parties, whether affectual or traditional,
that they belong together."[9]

Both Emile Durkheim and Max Weber employed the term
"solidarity" to describe the cohesiveness of a group which exhibits collective intentional behavior. Durkheim distinguished between cases
of mechanical and organic solidarity. In mechanical solidarity, the
individuals become totally integrated into the larger social whole and
can achieve collective action only by complete emersion in the group.
But, in organic solidarity, each individual need not lose his or her
identity in the group, for this type of solidarity actually arises out of
a division of labor. In mechanical solidarity, the individuals completely
lose their identities and become something like a collective being;
whereas in organic solidarity, the group is more effective the more
the individual members retain and develop their own individualities.[10]
For Durkheim, both types of solidarity engender a form of common
consciousness among group members.[11] This latter concept seems to
fit best the cases of mob action.

What has most interested sociologists is the way that some groups
are united together by factors such as solidarity without any organizational structure. What is crucial in the present context is that

sociologists have documented that some unorganized groups are able to display collective purposive conduct. Michael Brown and Amy Goldin use the Watts riots of 1965 to illustrate the sequence of episodes which result in collective behavior. They refer to the findings of the National Advisory Commission on Civil Disorders in describing the relevant facts.

> On the evening of August 11, as Los Angeles sweltered in a heat wave, a highway patrolman halted a young Negro driver for speeding. The young man appeared intoxicated and the patrolman arrested him. As a crowd gathered, law enforcement officials were called to the scene. A highway patrolman mistakenly struck a bystander with his billy club. A young Negro woman, who was erroneously accused of spitting on the police, was dragged into the middle of the street. When the police departed, members of the crowd began hurling rocks at passing cars, beating white motorists, and overturning cars and setting fire to them. The police reacted hesitantly. Action they did take further inflamed the people in the street.[12]

The situation continued to accelerate until full-scale looting and arson occurred a day later. The points of confrontation included both the altercations between police and crowd members and the hesitant response by the police to the initial violent outbursts of the members of the crowd.

When the people of Watts first took to the street, they were most probably motivated by what Sartre called the knowledge that they would find others who were of similar minds, yet these individuals also had other objectives which were "otherwise indeterminate."[13] Brown and Goldin characterized the background conditions that motivated these people as an "assault on a vulnerable and helpless community by a powerful representative of white colonial interests."[14] Once in the streets, the crowd became stimulated by various factors which brought about a certain result: what Brown and Goldin called the "crystallization of constructions" or, less metaphorically, a growing set of common beliefs and interests based on their similar situations and reactions to those situations. This is the beginning of group solidarity.

Sociologists have contended that there is plentiful evidence to show that collective consciousness produced by the sentiments of solidarity manifest a sort of intentionality. One sociologist, summarizing the results of several generations of research, said that the common theme running through all accounts of solidarity is that a "oneness" is achieved in certain groups.[15] This oneness or unity results from solidarity and allows for collective intentional action. In addition, other sociologists have claimed that purposiveness in a group is different from what it would be for individuals acting on their own. Several studies conducted by Bem, Wallach, and Kogan demonstrated that decisions and goals set by groups tended to be "more risky than decisions made by members as individuals."[16] Also, a number of studies show that for individuals in a cohesive group the goal of group success is an individual motivator which is independent of the goal of expected benefit to that individual.[17] And another study found that cohesive groups may come to accept states of affairs which would be considered suboptimal by the individual members if they were reaching decisions on their own.[18]

The intentions displayed by such social groups may be treated as if they were collective, since they arise out of the relations and structures of the group. The people in mobs could thus have intentions which drive them toward concerted action without being aware of having these intentions personally. Insofar as the memebers of a mob may be motivated to act to solve problems, their conduct can be seen as goal-directed and hence as meeting one of the commonly cited requirements of intentional conduct. But insofar as the members may not have reflective awareness of the purpose of their conduct, it is appropriate to say that these mob members display a pre-reflective or "quasi-intentional" state which motivates them to act in concert with one another. Being in a group which has achieved solidarity provides a catalyst to a kind of intentional action which can, in a limited way, be ascribed to the group.

While it is possible to attribute pre-reflective intentional action to individual members of mobs, it is also, in a limited sense, appropriate to attribute intentional action to the group, the mob, as well. If sociologists are correct in their empirical findings, the intentions and goals of some or most of the mob members are different from their intentions and goals as individuals. And while the change in their intentions is still a change in their individual intentions, it is the group structure that has brought about this change.

The new intentions can be attributed to the group in a limited way. But to say that there are collective intentions proper, that is, to say that the group can intend in just the same way that individual persons can intend, is a fiction. Rather each member of the group comes to have the same intention, either reflectively or pre-reflectively, and this is different from what their individual intentions would be if they were not members of the group. The sameness of intention is collective in the sense that it is caused by the group structure, that is, it is group-based. Thus, this more limited way of saying that there are collective intentions in a mob simply requires that there is evidence establishing that these intentions are group-based. I will have quite a bit more to say about concepts which are group-based, especially in chapter five.

II. Corporate Intent and Decision Procedures

Quite a lot of discussion in business ethics has concerned the question: Is the corporation a moral *person*? It seems to me that one can answer "no" to this question and still argue that it is appropriate to evaluate a corporation in moral terms. For corporate behavior to be assessed in moral terms, there must be intentional behavior which can be attributed to the corporation, but it need not be shown that the corporation is a moral entity in its own right. In order to show that intentions can be attributed in a limited sense to the corporation it is sufficient to show that the members of a corporation jointly engaged in purposive conduct. In addition, this purposiveness must be explained in terms of the structure of the corporation and cannot be reduced to the aggregated intentions of the individuals who compose the corporation.

In the previous section, I argued that the members of a mob behave in such a way as to display purposive conduct, but are not reflectively aware that they have such intentions. It is legitimate to speak of collective intent, in a limited sense, because these individuals are caused to act by the solidarity arising from the group, in ways they would not otherwise act and for goals they are not even aware of having. Corporations, unlike mobs, are among the most highly organized of groups. I will argue that decision procedures of a corporation combine and change the intentional states of key members of the organization so as to result in purposive behavior for the group.

For groups as divergent as mobs and corporations, I propose an analysis which rests on the same key feature in either case: the structure of the group makes it plausible to say that there are intentions which are group-based. In the case of mobs, this structure consists of group solidarity; in the case of corporations, the structure consists of the corporate decision-making structure. In both cases, purposive conduct of the group is ultimately explained by reference to the group structure which itself cannot be reduced to the aggregated intentions of the individual members of the group.

The chief reason for this lack of reducibility is that the structure of some social groups is important for a complete understanding of the intentions of the group. Explanations that fail to mention these structures cannot account for why these individuals act differently than they would on their own. Studies in management and social psychology indicate that individuals form intentions quite differently in corporations and in mobs than on their own. Indeed, in section I, I proposed that the intentional conduct displayed in mobs is a function of the felt solidarity within the mob rather than a function of the reflective awareness of each member of the mob. And in what follows here I will argue that the decision procedures of the corporation contribute greatly to the eventual shape of the consensus about the goals that the members of the corporation come to pursue. We must refer to the structure of the relationships which constitute these groups in order to give adequate explanations of the way that intentions are changed in these groups.

Solidarity in the mob and decision-making procedures in the corporation both change individual intentions in the sense that they create a group-based context for one's intentions that is radically different from the context of personal experience outside of the group. This group-based context is comprised of those social relationships among group members which form them into a group. And while it is obviously individuals who participate in these social relationships, the way that these relations or structures change and combine the intentions among these individuals cannot be fully explained by reference to the intentions of individual, isolated people. Like the channel of a river,[19] these social structures shape new intentions out of the previous intentions of individuals, and it is for this reason that it makes sense to talk, in a limited way, about the collective intent of social groups.

The limited ascription of collective intention is justified when individuals are related to each other in such a way that they come to have purposes and goals which are different from the purposes and goals they would have had on their own. In the case of corporate intent, these differences result from a formal organizational structure that assigns roles with special duties and also shapes a consensus out of the individual intents of board members. In the case of mob intent, these differences result from the informal structure which consists in the felt solidarity among group members. In both cases, the structure of the group provides a common basis for goal-directed activity. Insofar as the goals and purposes are group-based, it makes sense to ascribe limited collective intent to the social groups.

It is important to note that I do not claim that social groups manifest full-fledged collective intent, that is, they do not intend the joint actions they perform in the same way that individual persons intend their actions. In arguing that something social, namely the structure of the group, must be included in any explanation of the group's intent, I argue that statements about the group's intent cannot be fully captured by statements which are merely about the intentions of the individuals concerned. But I have not provided sufficient conditions for showing that groups intend their actions in the same way that individual persons intend theirs, for to do this I would have to show that social groups are the kind of entities that individual persons are. Instead, in what follows I indicate why I think that corporate intent is group-based, and hence is only to a limited extent a form of collective intent.

Organizational theorists and sociologists have provided empirical evidence for thinking that organizational structures have a powerful influence on the beliefs and decisions of the persons who are members of large-scale corporations. For example, Chris Argyris and Donald Schon claim that organizational structure affects the ability of individuals to learn and respond to changes in their environments. More importantly, they argue that individual learning, while necessary, is not sufficient for organizational learning to occur.

> We can think of organizational learning as a process mediated by the collaborative inquiry of individual members. In their capacity as agents of organizational learning, individuals restructure the continually

> changing artifact called organizational theory-in-use. Their work as
> learning agents is unfinished until the results of their inquiry — their
> discoveries, inventions and evaluations — are recorded in the media
> of organizational memory, the images and maps which encode organ-
> izational theory-in-use.[20]

According to Argyris and Schon, until the learning of one member
of an organization has been regularized in the organizational customs
and structures of decision making, the learning may be lost if the individual member should leave the organization. The new member
who replaces this departing member must have access to what was
previously learned for the initial learning to be truly an example of
organizational learning. And it is the way that various beliefs get
embedded in corporate decision-making structures that shows corporate learning and subsequent decision making to be group-based.

Sociologists have also documented the fact that members of highly
structured organizations develop different norms and mores as organization members than they would hold, or do hold, outside of a given
organizational setting. Gordon Donaldson and Jay W. Lorsch contend that "all of the beliefs in each company are a tightly interrelated
system" which is best characterized as a "fabric" or pattern of beliefs
"which do not exist in isolation as discrete principles. Rather they are
closely interwoven in managers' thought processes."[21] Donaldson and
Lorsch explain that this "fabric" of beliefs has a very strong impact
on any manager that comes under the sway of a given company's
organizational structure.

Corporate beliefs and goals also act as restraints on individual
decision making within corporations. The original goals of a company often continue to affect the decisions of managers long after the
original board members are gone. One business executive reported that

> in the beginning of the company [the founders] wanted to make cer-
> tain products, which led to a certain organization, which in turn led
> to our way of managing, which reinforced our products. It isn't the
> result of any intellectual process but it evolves.[22]

In a major study of 150 decisions in organized groups, a team of
organizational theorists from England concluded that organizational
structure played such an important role that it caused managers to
develop quite different types of decision making as they moved from

one organization to another. This effect is achieved because, they argued, "organization affects access to and authorization of decision making."[23]

Contrary to what individualists (both methodological and ontological) hold about such cases, there cannot be a complete reduction of the corporate intention to the individual, isolated intentions of the members (or even of key members) of the corporation. The structure of the corporation does make a metaphysical difference in that it causes changes in intent for the members of this social group, thereby warranting the ascription of limited intent to the corporation.

Peter French, defending a form of collectivism, has argued that "a Corporation's Internal Decision Structure (its CID Structure) provides the requisite redescription device that licenses the predication of corporate intentionality."[24] French correctly thinks that the key to corporate intentionality is to be found in the redescriptions of acts or intentions of individual persons as acts or intentions of corporations. French is also correct in thinking that it is the decision-making structure of the corporation that provides the warrant for this redescription. But French is mistaken to think that this decision-making structure warrants us to say that corporations are "intentional actors in their own right."[25]

What separates French's position from mine may seem to be minor, but it is not. We both agree that the decision-making structure of corporations allows one to speak of corporate intentions, that is, that the decision-making structures of a corporation warrant us to talk about new intentional states in the world. However, for French, these new intentional states partially warrant the claim that corporations are full-fledged intentional actors. By contrast, I reject the view that corporate intent must be the intent of some entity having moral agency in its own right.

My argument against French can be put quite succinctly by considering a hypothetical example of corporate decision making which is drawn from many similar real-life cases. After lengthy discussions, the board of directors of company X decides to pursue policy A, a compromise proposal. Prior to the board meeting, none of the board members wanted to pursue policy A. But during the meeting no other policies had the support of the majority of the board members. French claims that in such examples "the intentions and acts of various biological persons" are "subordinated and synthesized" into a "corporate decision."[26] For French, the metaphysical change in the nature of the intentions present in the boardroom warrants the redescription of the individual intentions as intentions of the corporate personality.[27] But a much simpler explanation of what has occurred is possible: *consensus* has been reached among the members of the board.[28] This is a kind of synthesis, but not one which creates new moral agents in their own right.

Such consensus-based goal setting, achieved through the corporate decision-making structure, cannot properly be conceptualized in terms of intentions of corporations that have metaphysical or moral status in their own right. The simplest way of showing this is that if enough board members subsequently change their minds about policy A, the corporation must follow suit. The consensus is a consensus of individuals, and when those individuals change their intentions, the corporate intention changes. French admits that corporate acts are causally inseparable from the acts of the individual members of that corporation. But he fails to see that this causal inseparability makes it implausible and unnecessary to posit independent corporate moral agency. It is not true that the intentions of the board members become intentions of some other entity instead of remaining the intentions of individual moral agents. Policy A became the policy of company X because it had already become the intentional policy of a majority of the individual board members. As a result, this policy can be described only in a very limited way as the intentional stance of company X.

While the notion of a corporation as a metaphysical or moral entity in it own right is not tenable, I still agree with French that the decision-making structure of a corporation does make a difference in that it does warrant the ascription of collective intent to the corporation, although in a quite limited way. Just as in the case of joint action described in chapter two, the organizational structure has facilitated behavior which would not have occurred if the individuals had acted on their own intentions in the absence of the corporate decision-making structure, and which cannot be fully understood apart from this structure. The intentions of the people who are employees, managers, and even board members, are changed by the corporate decision structure.

Thomas Donaldson has raised a significant challenge to those who support even a limited concept of corporate intentionality for the purposes of the moral evaluation of corporate behavior. He claims that it is not sufficient to show that a group of persons behaves intentionally, in the sense that there is purposiveness to what they do, in order for the kind of intentionality definitive of moral agency to be established for the corporation.

> A cat may behave intentionally when it crouches for a mouse. We know that it intends to catch the mouse, but we do not credit it with moral agency. . . . A computer behaves intentionally when it sorts through a list of names and rearranges them in alphabetical order, but we do not consider the computer to be a moral agent. Perhaps corporations resemble complicated computers; perhaps they, according to a complicated inner logic, function in an intentional manner but fail altogether to qualify as moral agents.[29]

French has less difficulty with this objection than I do, for as he has said in reply, it is merely the case that the cat and the computer behave as if they were acting intentionally. French maintains that corporations actually behave intentionally in the full-bodied human sense in that they are aware of and can modify their ways of behaving.[30] Since I do not follow French in thinking that corporations are full-bodied persons, in a sense I need not be bothered by the fact that I have not established that corporations are moral agents. But Donaldson's point runs deeper, for what he is challenging is the moral significance of attributing intentionality to corporations. I will try to explain why I wish to attribute even limited collective intent to corporations and other social groups on the basis of the fact that these social groups behave purposively, and why this attribution is morally significant.

Part of the reason for treating corporations as having intentions is, as Donaldson suggests, that corporations act as if they were pursuing goals. But it is also because corporate goals and decisions cannot be reductively explained by reference to individual persons. The same reductive point could not be made about the purposive behavior of cats and computers, for we can quite easily explain the appearance of goal-directed behavior in terms of instincts of cats and programs of computers. Initially then, I am making only an explanatory point: we need to make reference to the group in order to explain the purposiveness of behavior displayed in certain cases. The decision-making structures of corporations play a role in the setting of corporate policies and goals which means that one cannot reduce talk of corporate policies and goals to talk of the goals of the individual members of the corporation. As I said before, this gives us reason, on explanatory grounds, for saying that some corporate intentions are group-based.

The moral point is more complex. Action and intention are the two chief features commonly cited as necessary for moral evaluation. When both of these features can, even in a limited sense, be attributed to the group, then it is plausible to think that the group can also be the subject of moral evaluation. In the next chapter I defend the view that blame or fault can be attributed to groups, when action and intention have been attributed to these groups. In this chapter, I construct the case for claiming that some groups are negligent, rather than intentionally faulty, in their behavior. Sufficient conditions for negligent fault are much easier to establish than sufficient conditions for intentional fault when it is groups which are said to act. However, the moral evaluation of groups remains much more difficult to justify than the moral evaluation of individual human beings.

4. Collective Responsibility

The philosophical literature on collective responsibility is an interesting reflection of social and political turmoil in the world. In contemporary times the Nuremberg trials of the 1940s brought on the first wave of analysis of this concept,[1] and another wave followed the Eichmann trial of the early 1960s.[2] The greatest surge of interest occurred in response to the race riots and student demonstrations of the late 1960s.[3] A book of essays on collective responsibility by the leading moral philosophers of our day was published at the time of the public debate on the My Lai massacre in the early 1970s.[4] Since then there has been a sharp drop in scholarship about collective responsibility with the exception of work on corporate responsibility. In the 1980s some of my colleagues are again returning to the subject of collective responsibility of those groups which are not as highly organized as the corporation.[5]

In this chapter, I will draw on the discussion of the two previous chapters in order to argue that it is plausible to hold some groups, in a sense, collectively responsible for the harms caused by their members. In section I, I argue that mobs can be attributed sufficient power and intent to warrant holding them collectively responsible. In section II, I argue for a similar thesis concerning corporations, returning to the case of sexual harassment in the university. In section III, I consider the question of corporate criminal responsibility, and begin to ford the stream separating collective and individual responsibility. I end this section by making some suggestions about how punishment should be distributed against the members of corporations. Finally, in section IV, I briefly address the question of the distribution of criminal responsibility for mob members.

I. Mobs and Collective Responsibility

In this section I will argue that collective responsibility can be attributed to some mobs. I use the term "mob" to refer to social groups which have no decision-making or organizational structures, but which, unlike random crowds, have come together for economic or political reasons. It is generally held that mobs cannot be responsible because they do not have a decision-making structure. If there were a decision-making structure, then the actions of some members would become "vicarious" actions of the whole group. Similarly, the decisions made by some members about which actions to take would become the group's (vicarious) intent. Even though mobs do not have explicit decision-making structures, both action and intention are accomplished through the relation which binds the mob together, the solidarity among its members. Because of this solidarity, all of the mob members, in some cases, contribute to a given action — even the seemingly inactive members can be seen as vicariously related to the mob's action through their omissions. Similarly, solidarity allows the mob members to attain a kind of collective intention.

Mob members can contribute to harmful consequences caused by the mob in three ways. First, when some members are *instrumental* in a harmful action, they contribute directly. Second, when others *facilitate* such conduct, they contribute indirectly. And, third, when the rest of the members *fail to prevent* the harmful conduct of some members, these remaining members also contribute indirectly due to their negligence. In such cases it can then be said that all mob members causally contribute to a harmful collective action.

If there is also a collective intent involved in mob behavior, then it is not unfair to hold the whole group collectively responsible for the harm that occurs. One influential sociologist has described crowd behavior in the following way:

> There is a general agreement that a person who is a full member of a crowd, not a mere spectator watching from the periphery, is liable to behave differently from the way he would behave if he were by himself. This is so striking that some authors, such as Le Bon, one of the best known writers on the subject, feel inclined to postulate some kind of 'collective mind.' Such a hypothesis, [is] suggested no doubt by the homogeneity of the crowd.[6]

In this section I will also say a bit more about the homogeneity of intent that generally characterized mob behavior, while also trying to do justice to the fact that the members of the mob, if they were alone, would not necessarily have these intentions.

My account makes it a necessary condition for the ascription of collective responsibility to unorganized groups that each member of a group engage in acts or omissions which contribute to the harmful consequence for which the group is held collectively responsible. However, while each member must contribute in some respect (either through act or omission) in order for a group to bear collective responsibility for a harm, the contribution of each does not necessarily determine how individual responsibility will be distributed among the members. My account of the collective responsibility of mobs thus does not fall prey to the objection that collective responsibility is merely a form of strict liability, as I will briefly indicate at the end of this section.

First, then, it is my contention that the members of a mob can all be seen as contributing to a given harmful occurrence in one of three ways:

1. by direct causal contribution
2. by indirectly contributing through aiding or facilitating those directly involved
3. or by indirectly contributing through omissions.

If a mob member is able (alone or in combination with others) to prevent the group from causing harm, then, by failing to do so, that mob member contributes to any harm caused directly or indirectly by the other group members. And while such a contribution may be less important than the direct or indirect causal contributions of others, it is a contribution nonetheless. In what follows, I will concentrate on this last contribution (3) because it is the most controversial.

Alvin Goldman has argued that a person who is a member of a group has some power collectively with others in the group if there is a scenario such that this group member is a part of a subset of group members which could have brought about or prevented the whole group from doing a certain action.[7] In this sense, an individual member can be said to contribute to a group's action if that group member could have been a member of an efficacious subset of the whole group. The contribution may include such things as the failure of a given individual to aid in the formation of a subset which could have prevented a harm from being perpetrated by the group. Of course, these scenarios must be ones which could plausibly occur in the world at the time in question. This analysis by Goldman does justice to the intuitive idea that some omissions have moral weight and provides a way for deciding when omissions in social groups are morally relevant and when they are not.

However, it bears repeating that I am not claiming that possible contribution in an efficacious subset of a group is sufficient for *individual* moral responsibility. We are concerned only with the ascription of *collective* moral responsibility to groups of persons, and hence, this contribution, while important for collective responsibility, should not be seen as sufficient for the ascription of individual moral responsibility. Other conditions, especially related to the personal blameworthiness of the individual members, would also have to be present for the contributing individuals to be held individually responsible for the harm in question. In keeping with my middle position, I believe that collective responsibility does not reduce to the responsibility of individuals aggregated together.

One objection which might be raised against my view is that the mere counterfactual responsibility of being able to prevent a given outcome does not seem to be sufficient to establish the kind of contribution which has moral implications. Counterfactual possibility is a far cry from the kind of causal agency normally required for judgments of moral responsibility. The general question here is this: How are we to conceive of factors which facilitate, or as the lawyers say, provide an occasion for, another factor to operate so as to cause harm?

Hart and Honoré have written extensively on the question of what constitutes "contribution" on the part of one person to the action of another, and on the nature of what they call "occasioning" harm.[8] In both cases, one person's omission may be linked to another person's action if the omission played a necessary role in the production of a harm. An example of such an omission would be leaving a bank vault unlocked so that another person could remove money from that vault. But it also may include cases where, for example, a person fails to put up a fence which could have kept people away from dangerous machinery. In this second case, the contribution of the person who should have, but did not, put up a fence is a counterfactual condition, the omission to prevent others from doing harm. And in common law, these factors are given causal status sufficient to warrant, for certain purposes, the ascription of legal responsibility to those who omit to act in certain ways.[9]

Of course, in both legal and moral domains there must be some moral duty to prevent harm on the part of the person involved in order for the person's contribution to be relevant to an assessment of blame or fault. For blame or fault to be assigned there must be some preexisting reason for thinking that a given person should prevent a given harm from occurring. Only in such cases can it be claimed that an omission constitutes the kind of contribution to a result which is morally or legally relevant. Otherwise, people would have to spend all of their time trying to avoid omitting to do things which could conceivably contribute to harming someone in the world. The morality and legality of omissions is generally limited to that sphere where one's past conduct has created a reason for making one responsible for the actions and consequences of others.

Group membership changes a person's normal duties and responsibilities.[10] People join groups because the groups enable people to do things they could not otherwise do alone. By joining groups, individuals attain increased ability as a benefit, but there is also a corresponding cost: members have a special duty to prevent harms caused by their fellow group members, where such preventative acts do not risk significant harm to group members. When a mere bystander allows mob members to engage in harmful conduct, this omission is part of the normal expected background. But from the moral point of view, the same behavior on the part of a mob member would not be so considered because of the changed duties brought on by group membership. Hence, we have the following two-part analysis of how omissions count in the ascription of moral responsibility to mobs.

1. the omission contributed to the result
2. *and* the omission was not part of the normally existing background conditions.

This final analytical point allows us to distinguish the contribution of mob group members from the possible contribution of bystanders who also could have prevented a given harm.

There is a philosophical question which should be raised about this account. This question concerns the ability of mob members to affect the resulting group action. Consider the case in which a joint effort is called for, and the pool of candidates is overdetermined (or non-scarce). This means that there are more than enough people present to contribute to the joint venture. In moral philosophy, this scenario poses a difficulty because it is not clear that a given member of the group can prevent the group from doing other than what it does by withholding his or her contribution, since that member's contribution is not essential to the result. If those who share in collective responsibility had to be those who made essential contributions to the result, then the overdetermination would affect the assessment of their collective responsibility.

I will next more fully analyze the concept of individual *contribution* to a joint undertaking, in terms of both ability and intention. I will claim that the overdetermination of the group may weaken the argument for assigning collective responsibility, but not for those cases in which the members have a collective *intent* to contribute to the result. I will expand on the discussion in the previous chapter where I defended Sartre's attempt to understand the intentions of mob members.

The question of overdetermination can be partially answered by an analogy to joint omissions involving only two people. If I could have prevented a harm which you also could have prevented, what seems to count most is what each of us intended by failing to take preventive steps. If we both intended to enable a given result by failing to prevent it, then we are each individually responsible regardless of the fact that it only would have taken one of us to prevent the harmful result.

In the case of the omissions involved in mob action, similar although slightly different considerations obtain. Both ability and intent, for all members, are necessary for individual moral responsibility to be distributed throughout a mob; but if the intent is collective, the responsibility may be collective as well and need not distribute to the individuals.

In the novel *To Kill a Mockingbird*, a little girl is able to cause a mob to disband merely by engaging the mob members in discussion about their home lives. Atticus Finch, the girl's father, tries later to explain what had happened.

> "A mob's always made up of people, no matter what. Mr. Cunningham was part of a mob last night, but he was still a man. Every mob in every little Southern town is always made up of people you know — doesn't say much for them, does it?"
>
> "I'll say not," said Jem.
>
> "So it took an eight-year-old child to bring 'em to their senses, didn't it?" said Atticus. "That proves something — that a gang of wild animals

can be stopped, simply because they're still human. Hmp, maybe we need a police force of children . . . you children last night made Walter Cunningham stand in my shoes for a minute. That was enough."[11]

This example helps illustrate a point which Sartre made about pre-reflective consciousness, and also helps us begin to make sense out of the concepts of solidarity and collective intention as components in collective responsibility.

In the previous chapter, it was not claimed that all of the members of the mob have merely pre-reflective intentions. It may very well be that the leaders and other members of the mob have intentions which they are quite reflectively aware of. But many sociologists describe the apparently common phenomenon in which mob members behave in ways they wouldn't behave if they were alone. In the nineteenth century, Le Bon tried to explain this by saying that the behavior of mob members closely resembled the behavior of individuals under hypnosis.[12] Le Bon was not far off the mark. Hypnotic and mob behavior sometimes manifest a state of consciousness of which the person is not fully aware.

But unlike Le Bon, and following Sartre, I contend that there is a kind of pre-reflective conscious state for some mob members which is not a state of trance. This state may be intentional, unlike trances or frenzied behavior, without the specific members being reflectively aware of having these specific intentions. This explains why some members of mobs act quite differently in the mob than when alone and reflecting on their behavior. It is commonly held that when a person is in a hypnotic trance the person is not acting intentionally, since the person is not reflectively aware of his or her intentions and the behavior is out of the person's control. It is the factor of control which distinguishes the person in a hypnotic trance from the person who is in a state of pre-reflective consciousness. Since the element of control remains, the state of pre-reflective consciousness can be characterized as at least *quasi*-intentional.

There are important moral implications of Sartre's view. He has provided us with a plausible phenomenological account of a state of consciousness that is motivational and yet not reflective. From the moral point of view, the acts which result from these intentions are not subject to individual blame, since the individuals are not aware of having the intentions. But the acts may be subject to collective blame, especially if the intentions can be plausibly said to be a function of membership in a given group.

The description of the break-up of the mob in *To Kill a Mockingbird* illustrates the pre-reflective intentions that occur in a mob. The mob broke up because its members were forced to reflect on themselves as individual persons. Previously, the members were lost in their feelings of solidarity, by a kind of anonymity which comes from *merely* being members of a group. In this context, one might think about the practice in some groups of shielding individual members' identities, through, for example, the use of uniforms or facial hoods. It may be that in some cases, this shielding of personal identity also aids in suppressing each individual member's awareness of his or her own unique personal identity. As soon as Atticus Finch's daughter started identifying each of the mob members as individuals in their own rights, by referring to past private conversations or to the deeds of their children, the mob members could no longer suppress their own personal awareness and identify themselves merely as mob members. They again became people who were personally aware of themselves and what they were doing.

The members of the mob in *To Kill a Mockingbird* were trying to accomplish various tasks, and as such they were displaying intentions and goals in their behavior. The mob members did not seem to be acting as automatons or in a frenzied trance, and hence their actions, and the actions of similar mobs, may be the proper subject of moral responsibility ascriptions of some sort. It is best to conceive of the responsibility of mobs in collective terms because the very intent to act comes from a sense of solidarity which the members feel toward each other, perhaps as the result of recognizing a common enemy.

Of crucial importance in the analysis of group actions taken by mobs are the relationships that exist among the members of these groups. Since there are no formal decision-making procedures, the cohesiveness of a mob, and hence its ability to engage in joint undertakings, is not straight-forwardly a function of its organization. Rather, such factors as common interests and shared beliefs about one's identity as a member of a group, as well as historical events such as the existence of a common enemy or oppressor, create a complex structure for the mob. These factors may be effective at bringing the group together in a state of solidarity. In such cases, the relationships that exist among the members may unify the group and allow for joint actions, and these relationships are the crucially important factors for the eventual ascription of responsibility to the group.

As was argued earlier, the solidarity felt by each member creates either reflective or pre-reflective intentions within the mob members that enable these mob members to engage in concerted action. Here we have the intentional basis for the contributions of each member of the group to any harmful result for which the group is collectively responsible, that is, the solidarity relationships that allowed each member to aid others in joint action. Each member, to varying degrees, aids each other member. Even those members who do not directly cause or indirectly facilitate the harmful act, share in the collective responsibility for it because they could form a subgroup to prevent the ensuing harm by withdrawing their aid or by actively opposing the others. And it is membership in the mob that, in the first place, gives to each member the special duty to prevent the mob from doing harm, a duty which comes with the ability that these members have to engage in efficacious joint action.

The pre-reflective intentions of the mob members can be best described as collective intentions since the members of the mob collectively carry out various actions which require both motivation and intention. The ability to engage in collective action is due to the solidarity of these members, and it is this solidarity which distinguishes the moral status of the mob members from that of the bystanders who happen to be in the vicinity of the mob. The bystanders are nothing but individuals who happen to be standing in a given spatial location. They have no special relationships to mob members simply in virtue of being there, and, thus, no special duties to prevent the mob from doing harm.[13] The mob members, though, are related by their solidarity and normally this is most evident when the mob has formed for political or economic reasons. It is then that there arises a common interest of the mob members which allows them to engage in concerted action, and which is the basis of their special duties for the actions of the mob as a whole.

The members of the group may act intentionally without necessarily being reflectively aware of having explicit intentions to so act. Since there is intentional action occurring, without individual reflective awareness of it, and since features of the group seem to make the intentional action possible, either through the actions or omissions of the group members, I contend that it is best to characterize such intentional acting as, in a sense, collective. One reason for viewing things in this way comes from the disparity that exists between the norms for individual, personal conduct, which are held by mob members, and the norms these same persons hold when in groups. The members of the mob in *To Kill a Mockingbird* were tolerant of certain conduct when they were in a mob, although the sociological evidence of similar events suggests that not all members were reflectively aware of this. Yet at the same time, these mob members held personal norms which turned out to be incompatible with the attitudes they held while members of the group. It is for this reason that the mob disbanded when the members were forced to become reflectively aware again of themselves as distinct individuals.

H. D. Lewis argued in a 1948 article that the notion of collective responsibility was simply "barbarous" because it held one person responsible for the action of another person.[14] Lewis actually made a category mistake in his argument, since truly collective responsibility does not make any person individually responsible; rather, it is the group which is said to be responsible. The "barbarity" only arises, if at all, when the ascription of collective reponsibility is parsed in terms of the individual responsibilities of the members of the group.

Many other authors have objected to the concept of collective responsibility since it is seen as a form of strict liability — that is, collective responsibility is said to be a form of responsibility which does not look to the actual contributions made by each of the members of a group. Joel Feinberg defines collective responsibility as a subspecies of strict liability because he believes that in collective responsibility the condition of contributory fault is weakened or eliminated.[15] But, as we have seen, collective responsibility can take into account the specific contributions made by each member of the group.

Feinberg distinguishes between distributional and nondistributional responsibility for groups, and he claims that these two categories are mutually exclusive. It seems to me, though, that collective responsibility is not captured by either of these categories. In distributional responsibility, there is little gained by speaking of the group at all, for it is possible to parse the group's responsibility completely in terms of what each and every member of the group would have been responsible for on his or her own in any event. Both Feinberg and I believe that collective responsibility is quite different from distributional responsibility. Feinberg thinks that collective responsibility is a form of strict liability since it involves nondistributional responsibility. Here, the group membership does make a difference — one could not understand the responsibility of the group merely by understanding what each member of the group would have been responsible for on his or her own. But this lack of reducibility does not mean that the contributions of each member to the end result are eliminated (or even rendered weak or unimportant). It is for this reason that I do not regard collective responsibility as a form of nondistributional responsibility either. What is vitally important is that each member contributed to the actions of the others, and that only by joint contribution and collective intent was the concerted action possible.[16]

Thus, the members of mobs have the two chief characteristics which are necessary for the ascription of moral responsibility: participation and intention. But since the intention is not a reflective state for most members, the members of mobs should not be held individually responsible for the harms caused by them. Rather, collective moral responsibility is, in a sense, the appropriate category to apply to mobs. (I have here skirted the difficult question of how moral blame should be meted out against the members of a mob, being content merely to establish that collective moral responsibility is an appropriate category to apply to mobs.) And while this does not entail distributional responsibility, it may be that some members of the mob, especially those who take a leadership role within the mob, may be singled out for individual blame and punishment. I will return to this subject in section IV of the present chapter.

II. Corporate Responsibility

In this section, I will set out my own model of corporate responsibility, delineating its strengths and weaknesses. This analysis will then be applied to the case of sexual harassment which I first set out in the Introduction. Later, in section III, a detailed case analysis of corporate criminal responsibility will be presented in which I will elaborate on the theory of corporate responsibility and draw analogies to conspiracies and employer misconduct in criminal law. I will sketch an alternative model of collective responsibility, and I will show that it is better able to deal with the most common cases involving harms attributed to corporations. The present section will also clarify why I think that Joel Feinberg has not given an adequate conceptualization of collective responsibility.

It has seemed to some that we have only two theoretical models open to us for assigning corporate responsibility. Either we can treat corporations the same way that we treat individual persons in criminal law, by looking to the corporation's state of mind, conduct, and the consequences of its acts, or we can treat corporations as strictly liable for whatever results from their "actions" regardless of the state of mind or faultiness of conduct, as is sometimes done in tort law. The first strategy is attractive because it calls for no major change in our general view of moral or legal responsibility and comports well with the long tradition of speaking of corporate persons. The second strategy is attractive because it avoids the considerable evidentiary problems of the first strategy, that is, finding the corporate mind and will and separating it from the minds, wills, and conduct of the individual members of the corporation. We are faced, however, with a severe problem with each alternative. The first strategy seems inappropriate in most corporate cases since it rests on an analogy which fails to distinguish solitary actions from joint actions, that is, actions involving only one person from actions involving a group of persons. The second strategy is inappropriate as a way of assigning moral or legal responsibility since it seems to deny our intuitions that blameworthiness or fault is a necessary condition of responsibility.

Clearly there is no reason to think that these are the only models of responsibility open to us, nor even that these are the models best suited to the peculiar characteristics of the corporation. These two models show us, though, what is needed in another model. What we need are models of responsibility aimed at collectivities, but where the blame or fault condition is preserved as a condition or responsibility. One such model can be constructed by combining the concepts of vicarious agency with negligent fault.

Corporate vicarious negligence is that model of responsibility which seems, in cases of corporate responsibility for employee wrongdoing, to best function as a mean between these two extremes of strict liability and individual intentional wrongdoing. The causal condition of corporate vicarious negligence is that of vicarious agency. I shall define vicarious action to be action "a" done by "y" but attributable to "x." Such attribution is normally due to such facts as that "y" has been delegated to do "a" as a substitute for, or representative of, "x."

Negligent fault is the fault condition most appropriate to the majority of cases with which a theory of corporate responsibility must deal. If a corporation is said to act, the question always remains: Wasn't it merely an act of an individual person who only happened to be a member of that corporation? With negligence, though, if it is said that the corporation failed to perform an action (which was required by a duty it had), the question does not arise. Since the corporation can only act through one of its members, a failure of every one of the members to act will become a failure of the corporation to act; whereas, an action of a single member of a corporation does not necessarily become that corporation's action.

Here is one model of corporate vicarious negligence which sets sufficient conditions for the harmful conduct of a member of the corporation to become the responsibility of the corporation.

> A corporation is vicariously negligent for the harmful acts of one of its members if:
> a) causal factor — the member of the corporation was enabled or facilitated in his or her harmful conduct by the general grant of authority given to him or her by a corporate decision; and
> b) fault factor — appropriate members of the corporation failed to take preventive measures to thwart the potential harm by those who could harm due to the above general grant of authority, even though:
> 1. the appropriate members could have taken such precautions, and
> 2. these appropriate members could reasonably have predicted that the harm would occur.

The major advantage of the model I am proposing is that the corporation is treated not as a single entity but as a collection of entities or persons, some of whom grant authority to others, some of whom might harm others, and some of whom might act to minimize the potential of harm. Most, if not all, cases of supposedly harmful corporate conduct involve some sort of collective action, resembling a conspiracy of individual persons with more than one person acting on his or her own. The link between these persons is often hard to establish, but in most cases the definitive link between an individual and a corporate representative occurs due to an omission rather than a commission. For example, the person who is designated by the group to be the supervisor of the actions of an employee of the corporation fails to take action to thwart the harmful acts of that employee. This failure to act links the corporation to the harmful practice of the employee. If this is true, then a model of corporate responsibility and liability directed at vicarious negligence would be best suited to the realities of corporate life.

The second general advantage of the model I am proposing is that it is likely to be more effective than other models of corporate liability, especially strict liability. Corporate officers will see that there is a clear way to rebut the charge that the corporation is liable for a particular harm. It can be shown that (1) either the corporation did not authorize its member to engage in the type of conduct that produced the harm, or (2) even though its member was generally authorized to so act, the corporation took reasonable measures to prevent the occurrence of that harm. This knowledge would tend to deter future harms since the corporate officers will not feel as powerless as they do under standards of strict liability to affect the future liability of the corporation.

One might think that the main disadvantage of this alternative to intentional wrongdoing and strict liability is that it shifts the legal burden away from the corporation by increasing the number of excuses to which a corporation can appeal. I can't deny that this model of corporate responsibility would add several special excuses to those presently open to the corporation — excuses which show that due care was exercised by the corporation, for example, in a hiring policy or supervisory policy, and thus whatever harm resulted is the responsibility of the individual not the corporation of which that individual is a member. The availability of these special excuses, though, is quite likely to make corporations more careful in the establishment of their policies, especially where potentially harmful conduct is concerned.

Finally, it might be objected that what I have been calling vicarious negligence is not vicarious liability at all, as presently conceived in legal circles. Again, I must plead guilty to this charge. It has become commonplace to define vicarious liability as a form of strict liability, hence ruling out negligence, or any other fault condition, by definition. The notion of vicarious responsibility, or perhaps more properly vicarious "agency," that I have employed differs significantly from that which Joel Feinberg and others employ in legal theory.[17] But the kind of vicarious responsibility I have in mind is not out of keeping with the commonsense understanding of what "vicarious" means. Perhaps this thesis is even more radical than one would otherwise think, for the claim that all corporate conduct is vicarious flies in the face of the fiction in legal theory of corporations as full-fledged legal persons. As I argued in chapter one, this fiction should be dispensed with, unless a clear referent of the fiction can be found in the world. What we should be concerned with is whether there is a structural feature of the corporation which has allowed for a nexus of actions taken by the members of a corporation. Responsibility or liability should be assigned to a corporation when that nexus of actions which cause a harm can be properly attributed to the corporation.

Irving Thalberg and others have contended, by way of a thought-experiment, that if all human beings perish, it would be absurd to say that there would still be corporations acting in the world. This indeed is the central insight that stimulated me to look for a way of describing corporate agency which is dependent on the acts of individual human beings. Corporations are not independent agents because, unlike human beings, they could not act without other human beings acting. The concept of acting through another or vicariously acting is meant to capture this insight. This type of agency is similar to that which occurs in the legislative process where the act of one (or a number of) individual(s) is redescribed as the act of a group. What is the causal nexus that warrants one to redescribe an act of a human being as an act of a corporation? The case of sexual harassment mentioned in the introduction illustrates the difference between acts of human beings *simpicitor* and acts of human beings which, for the purpose of assigning responsibility, can be described as corporate acts.[18]

Professor Smith calls in one of his graduate students, Ms. Jones, and says "I'd like you to sleep with me. If you won't, I'll make sure you lose your assistantship." Now, can this personal encounter between two human beings be redescribed so that Y University is said to be responsible for the harassment of one of its students? Here is one set of facts for which it could plausibly be held that Y University is responsible for the actions of Professor Smith. The Board of Trustees of Y University voted favorably on a bill creating the office of university professor of philosophy. The job description said that anyone holding this office could teach as a university professor and advise and evaluate graduate students in philosophy. Anyone holding the office of philosophy professor was to be supervised respectively by the Chairman of Philosophy, the Dean of Humanities, and the Vice President for Academic Affairs. Those supervising the holder of this office could further stipulate appropriate conduct on the part of the office-holder, in this case, Professor Smith. Assume that in this instance, Professor Smith had threatened graduate students before, and word of this travelled to the Chairman, the Dean, and the Vice President, yet they had said nothing to Professor Smith or to any of his graduate students.

It seems clear that Mr. Smith could have made similar threats to graduate students attending Y University, but those threats would not be described as the threats of a professor of Y University if certain necessary conditions had not been met by the Board of Trustees, the Vice President, the Dean, and the Chairman. (I leave aside the point that the threat would probably have little effect without these conditions being met.) If Mr. Smith weren't employed by Y University, the event in question could not be described as Professor Smith harassing one of his students, and then Y University could not be held responsible for the harassment of one of its students by Professor Smith.

Notice that no one told Smith to harass student Jones and no member of the corporate entity, Y University, straightforwardly caused Smith to harass Jones. In fact, Smith could have tried to harass Jones whether Y University existed or not. But the corporate responsibility for the event occurred because of an action by the Board of Trustees and several acts of omission, negligent omissions at that.[19]

What might have broken the "causal nexus" such that the responsibility could not be ascribed to the university? Professor Smith's Chairman could have forbidden Smith to threaten his students, the Dean could have threatened to dismiss Smith from the graduate faculty, the Vice President could have threatened to dismiss Smith from the University if he didn't stop threatening his students. Any of these acts might disassociate the University from Smith's actions, as a recall petition would disassociate a constituency from the acts of a congressman. The commissions and omissions of the Trustees, the Vice President, the Dean, and the Chairman facilitate Smith's act and thereby link the corporation, Y University, to Smith's act. The acts of these people are the sufficient conditions for the ascription of corporate responsibility for Smith's acts. Contrary to the contention of John Ladd and others,[20] there is nothing in principle which limits corporate responsibility or liability to actions for which moral or legal responsibility would be normally inappropriate. I will have a great deal more to say about this subject, especially concerning the topics of omission and intent within corporations, in the next section.

III. Corporate Criminality

In 1975 the United States Supreme Court upheld a lower court ruling that John R. Park, the president of Acme Markets Inc., was criminally liable for "causing adulteration of food which had traveled in interstate commerce and which was held for sale."[21] In this section I will argue that it is proper to hold a corporation criminally liable or responsible for such acts, and that when such a determination has been made it may also be justifiable for criminal sanctions to be imposed on the chief executive officer of the corporation in question. First I will attempt to explain why it is plausible to assign corporate criminal responsibility for acts which were performed by individual persons, and then explain why it is justifiable to assign liability to members of that corporation who were not those who most directly participated in the criminal act (*actus reus*). In setting out my theoretical position I will be guided by analogies to the way in which conspiracies and employers are treated in criminal law. Here the less active party must have played some important role, perhaps precisely by remaining inactive and thereby acquiescing in the final result. Second, I will attempt to rebut the standard arguments against holding a corporation criminally liable for the actions of its employees. And finally I will explain why I think that punishing chief executive officers for the criminal actions of their corporations is a strategy preferable to two alternative approaches, both of which attempt to penalize the whole corporation. But before turning to those specific arguments, I will describe briefly the facts of *United States* v. *Park* to illustrate the kind of case to which the following theoretical analysis is designed to be applied.

Acme Markets, Inc. was shown to have received food that had

been shipped in interstate commerce. While this food was being stored in one of Acme's Baltimore warehouses, Acme employees caused the food "to be held in a building accessible to rodents and to be exposed to contamination by rodents."[22] The corporation admitted guilt in the adulteration of food which it then sold. This admission was based largely on two facts: that the food had been adulterated in the corporation's warehouse, and that the corporation's supervisory employees did not prevent this adulteration, even though the unsanitary conditions of the warehouse were well known to them. The acts of the employees were duly authorized and well within the job descriptions of the employees, and the supervisory negligence contributed to the criminal result thereby linking the corporation to these employees' acts. Thus, the corporation itself was guilty of a criminal offense.

John R. Park, as president of Acme Markets, Inc., had been notified about the unsanitary conditions at his Baltimore warehouse by the Food and Drug Administration after two different inspections of the warehouse by the Chief of Compliance of the F.D.A.'s Baltimore office. Park argued, though, that he was not personally concerned in this Food and Drug violation. Furthermore, he claimed that he was only "in a sense" responsible for the actions of the employees of the corporation. He was responsible for picking good underlings and supervisors, but not responsible for all of the actions that those employees engaged in. During cross-examination, Park "conceded that providing sanitary conditions for food offered for sale to the public was something that he was 'responsible for in the entire operation of the company.' " He also "admitted that the Baltimore problem indicated the system for handling sanitation 'wasn't working perfectly.' " Nonetheless, he continued to claim that he had done all that could be reasonably expected of him by assigning "dependable subordinates" to the task of supervising the correction of the sanitation problem when he was made aware of it by the F.D.A.[23]

The majority opinion of the Supreme Court argued that it was well established in criminal law as applied to corporations that those who are responsible for the commission of a misdemeanor "are limited to all who . . . have . . . a responsible share in the furtherance of the transaction which the statute outlaws." The court felt that it was up to the jury to determine who in each case stood in this responsible position in a given corporation. In this case, the Supreme Court reaffirmed its decision in *U.S.* v. *Dotterweich* (1943) in "holding criminally accountable the persons whose failure to exercise the authority and supervisory responsibility reposed in them by the business organization resulted in the violation complained of."[24] Specifically, it was recognized that the purpose of the Food and Drug Act was to punish "neglect where the law requires care, or inaction where it imposes a duty." Most importantly for my analysis, the Court held that "the failure to fulfill the duty imposed by the interaction of the corporate agent's authority and the statute furnishes a sufficient causal link" between Park and the criminal act of adulteration.[25] As even the author of the dissenting opinion recognized: "This is the language of negligence, and I agree with it."[26] For it was recognized by all that this negligence rendered Park criminally liable in a way which was not in conflict with moral intuitions, since his criminal guilt was thus based on his contribution to the criminal result.

The best way to conceive of corporate actions is on the model of vicarious agency,[27] or to simplify slightly, corporate actions are really only very complex arrangements of joint and vicarious actions of individual persons. On this way of understanding things, corporate responsibility is a type of collective responsibility, albeit a rather complex type. In the present section, two analogies will be developed which help explain this view. The analogy of conspiracies helps explain how it is that joint criminal actions are to be conceived; and the analogy of two-person companies, involving employer and employee, helps explain how the criminal actions of one person can be vicariously attributed to another person. Both analogies make reference to examples in the criminal law and set the stage for the defense of the view that corporations can be held criminally liable or responsible for the actions of corporate employees.

Joel Feinberg has discussed a theoretically interesting case of joint action. In some situations group members facilitate the actions of other group members in such a way that these others are enabled to do things that they could not do on their own. A group action in which the actions of some are dependent on the actions (or the failures to act) of others is called a conspiracy. Feinberg clearly explains why this is really a type of collective responsibility. He notes that "one may be guilty as an accessory, even of crimes one is not competent to perpetrate."[28]

Consider the case of E who hires D to make and set an explosive device in the car of F. Both E and D are guilty of conspiring to use explosives for an unlawful purpose. And this result is true, regardless of the fact that E could not have made or set the explosives on his own, and regardless of the fact that D would not have made the explosive device if it weren't for E's offer of money. This second point will turn out to be quite important in the analysis of corporate criminal responsibility, for it normally turns out that individual employees would have much less motivation to engage in potentially harmful conduct if they were not asked to do so and given sufficient monetary incentive.

The example of conspiracy illustrates well how it is that a group of persons can be said to have acted as a group, each facilitating, or contributing to, the overall result.[29] This example also illustrates how it is that a member of a group of this sort can be held to be at least partially responsible for a result even though it is not the result which he or she could or would have caused on his or her own. First, the conspiracy example shows how a collection of acts of individuals could be described as the act of a group. Each individual played some role either by engaging in some action (robbing the bank teller) or by failing to act at an appropriate time (failing to push the alarm button), and the various acts and omissions depended on one another for the result. Second, even though it is now the group which is said to be responsible for a crime (guilty of robbing the bank), one may look for ways of dissolving the group responsibility into the individual responsibilities of the members of the group. I will talk at length about this later on. Suffice it here to note that once group responsibility has been assigned, the further distribution of the responsibility to individuals need not be based on the actual causal roles initially played by these group members in the commission of the group act (perhaps the one who planned it all is held most responsible even though he merely observed the others rob the bank). This will become more clear when we consider group acts which are based on the kind of hierarchical relations that exist in business companies.

The collective efforts of several people in the commission of a crime are sometimes discussed under the category of vicarious responsibility, specifically concerning masters and servants or employers and employees. In civil law, especially the law of torts, a master can be held responsible for the actions of his or her servant. This legal policy was originally adopted in the late Middle Ages because there was more in the purse of the master than in that of the servant. It was more likely that the master could pay; but also the master was connected to the servant, since the master had the duty to supervise the servant. In more recent times, employers have sometimes been held responsible for the actions of their employees, when these employees acted within the scope of their employment. It has been quite controversial, though, whether a similar analysis is appropriate for holding the employer liable for the criminal acts of his or her employee.

A 1943 opinion in a Minnesota case clarifies the reluctance of legal scholars to let the doctrine of *respondeat superior*, as the doctrine of vicarious responsibility is known, be applied to criminal cases.

> Ordinarily the doctrine of *respondeat superior* has no application in criminal cases. Criminal liability, except for certain statutory offenses, and others not here material, is based upon personal guilt. Responsibility for the crimes of others rests upon causation. A defendant is held criminally liable for having counselled, procured, commanded, incited, authorized, or encouraged another to commit a particular crime. At the very time the rule of *respondeat superior* was being developed as a basis for vicarious civil liability it was rejected as a ground for similar criminal liability.[30]

Unless there is some personal involvement on the part of the master or employer, such as those listed above, the guilty state of mind (*mens rea*) is thought to be missing from the employer's act hence making it improper to hold him or her criminally liable. In civil law, on the other hand, such guilty involvement was not regarded as a necessary condition for responsibility on the part of the employer or master.

This brings us to the question of contributory guilt. For establishing criminality, it is not sufficient that a person play a causal role in the production of a crime. Rather, one must also be guilty in the way in which one acts, and this condition is different from the mere role one plays in a given relationship or organization. Nonetheless, there are many well-accepted cases where employers have been held criminally responsible for the acts of their employees. Consider the following two cases.

> A chauffeur had a fatal traffic accident as a result of his unlawful driving with criminal negligence. The employer, who was in the car at the time, observed the very improper driving and had ample opportunity to order the use of proper care but failed to do so, was also guilty of manslaughter.[31]

Over an extended period of time employees took and carried away the property of another and appropriated it to the use of their employer. The employer, who knew about this and took advantage of it without protest was guilty of larceny although the employees innocently believed it to be his property.[32]

Both of these cases involve contributory guilt on the part of the employer. In the first case there is the negligence of the employer, that is, the failure of the employer to fulfill his duty to supervise his employee's conduct, and thus to try to stop his chauffeur from driving with improper care. For this to be truly a case of contributory negligence, the employer had to know or should have known what his chauffeur was doing (or likely to do), and the employer had to have a previously assumed duty to supervise the conduct of the employee which was now not being fulfilled. In the second case, there is more than just negligence on the part of the employer. The employer is able to manipulate the ignorance of his employees. Now, while it is true that the manipulation was quite subtle and involved passive rather than active participation in the crime on the part of that employer, it is no less a form of manipulation. The employees are the employer's unwitting agents in crime. This point is also crucial for the theory of corporate criminal responsibility.

Corporations resemble conspiracies in that there is a common agreement among a group of people to engage in a certain type of behavior toward a certain end. Of course, normally corporations aim at what is legal, and conspiracies (by definition) aim at what is illegal. But it may happen that the possibility of illegal behavior exists even within what is normally a legal enterprise. And when a given supervisor or executive is, or should be, aware of the possibility, and yet does nothing to minimize this likelihood of harm, then that person is also implicated in the illegal or criminal act. This occurs when it is shown that the supervisor or executive facilitated the perpetration of the act by his or her acquiescence, and that the supervisor or executive had been put in the position of having the duty of watching and directing the activities of the employee. Thus, just as in the conspiracy case, other members of the corporation may be responsible for acts they did not and perhaps even could not do on their own.

Corporations resemble, perhaps much more clearly, the kind of employment situations in which an employer is held to be vicariously responsible for the actions of his or her employee. It should be obvious that corporations are involved in employment, but it is difficult to identify who precisely is the employer. The corporations themselves, and often their chief officers, are held civilly responsible for the actions of these employees. Yet, as in the case of simple employment relations, quite a controversy has arisen about whether corporations should be held criminally liable for the actions of their employees. The *Acme* case shows why it is that high-ranking members of a company are sometimes the ones who are held to be most responsible for corporate criminality even though their roles do not seem to be as active as those of the lower-ranking employees of the company. The Acme employees who allowed rodent infestation at the Baltimore warehouse were in some sense those most directly involved in the adulteration of the food. Yet, these employees could not have accomplished this result on their own. They had to have been hired and then placed in positions of responsibility over sanitation at the warehouses by high-ranking members of Acme, and ultimately approved by Mr. Park. Furthermore, all of those persons in the organizational chart who are supervisory to these employees are likely at least to acquiesce in the commissions and omissions of the Baltimore warehouse employees. While it is the Acme company that is the employer of these warehouse employees, the functions of a normal individual employer (defining of job descriptions, hiring of employees, supervising, etc.) were filled by high-ranking members of the company such as Mr. Park. Mr. Park had specific duties as a result of his role as president, just as is true for employers in small companies. If it sometimes makes sense to hold employers responsible for the actions of their employees because of the facilitating roles played by employers when they fail in their supervisory duties, then it also sometimes makes sense to hold supervisory or high-ranking members of a corporation responsible for the harms that the employees of that corporation cause.

For most ascriptions of corporate responsibility, negligence will play a central role. There will be many members of the corporation who, as in any other group, do not directly participate in the wrongful conduct of some of the other members. More importantly, it often happens that there are no important or high-ranking members of the corporation who actively participate in the wrongful conduct which some employee or other engages in. In fact, corporate officers, board members, and supervisors do not routinely participate directly in any of the actions taken by these employees. There will rarely be any smoking guns held by board presidents or even by supervisors. But the roles held by these high-ranking managers create duties to prevent harm by those lower-ranking employees who directly act for the corporation. The high-ranking managers are supposed to fulfill the employer roles for the corporation. When these roles are not carried out properly, then negligence has occurred among the 'employers,' and the corporation, as well as these high-ranking managers, is linked to the acts of the employees.

Corporate responsibility is much more complex than that involved in either conspiracies or simple two-person employment relations. For an act to be ascribed to the corporation there must be a decision made by high-ranking managers within the corporation and there must be an action taken by at least one of the employees of the corporation pursuant to that decision. Corporate responsibility then will also have two components: an act of an employee who is designated to act for the corporation, and some decision or other made by a high-ranking manager which facilitated the employee's act. It most often happens that the high-ranking manager's decision is a decision not to interfere or effectively to acquiesce in the behavior of the employee, thereby facilitating the employee's conduct. Such acquiescence would not be sufficient to link the corporation to the act of the employee, unless it were the manager's duty to act to prevent the employee from doing harm, for only then would the manager's act be negligent. This negligence would link the corporate decision-makers with the employee's acts, which would now fall under the description of the corporate action for which corporate responsibility could be assigned.

In the paradigm cases of criminal liability it must be shown that a given person has engaged in a criminal act (*actus reus*) with a guilty mind (*mens rea*). I will next confront the most frequently raised objections against the model of corporate responsibility I have been developing when that model is applied to cases of criminality. One objection to this model of corporate responsibility maintains that the criminal act (*actus res*) cannot be properly transferred from the employee to the corporation. Another objection maintains that the corporation cannot have the requisite state of guilty mind (*mens rea*) for criminal responsibility. And a third maintains that it is unfair to hold the corporation criminally responsible merely because its employees have been shown to have acted criminally.

Since most crimes are defined as offenses by one human being against another, and since the corporation is not a human being, it has been claimed that a corporation cannot engage in criminal conduct. Put a different way, if the *actus reus* must involve a human act, then the corporation cannot commit criminal acts. Perkins gives a definitive argument against this position.

> The court then concluded that a corporation cannot be guilty of manslaughter, overlooking entirely that the corporation can do nothing except by aid of human beings, and there never could be a case in which a corporation has killed a human being who was not killed by a human being.[33]

Corporations cannot act at all except vicariously, that is, through the actions of human beings who are their agents or employees. All corporate acts involve human acts. Unless it is held that corporations never act at all, it cannot be held that corporations could not commit acts such as killing, for corporations can kill just as they can make various products, that is, through the involvement of human employees who are authorized to act in this way.

There is a more serious question connected with the application of *actus reus* to corporations: When should a given act performed by a human being be attributed to the corporation? If a corporation is to be convicted of a crime, it must be established that the corporation was in some sense the perpetrator of the act. If the employee acted within his or her job description, then the act was authorized. In criminal law, the question is whether authorization literally transfers act ascription from one person to the corporation. Glanville Williams argues that authorization is not sufficient for this kind of ascription because it does not necessarily bring the master (or the corporation) within the definition of the proscribed act of a statute. In other words, a statute may specify that it is a crime to "enter" or "make" a certain thing, yet these acts could not be attributed to a master when engaged in by a servant or employee without moving far from the express words of the statute and thereby holding someone guilty for a crime that wasn't committed by that person. Just because I authorize you to enter into a certain area does not mean that I should be viewed as entering into that area. Williams contends that crimes are quite different from torts in this respect: authority does not transfer the *actus reus* from the servant to the master (or from the employee to the corporation).

What underlies Williams' demurrer is that vicarious criminality seems to offend against the principle that one person should not be penalized for the actions of another. The violation of this principle is seen to be unfair and morally "odious."[34] I would contend though that things are quite different when the individuals assume the corporate roles of high-ranking manager and employee. The acts of some employees are, and must be, describable as the acts of the corporation if the corporation can act at all. The acts of corporate lawyers are treated as acts of the corporation in the making of contracts, etc. Similarly, corporations involve complex actions and relations that sometimes warrant treating the corporation as the criminal agent when its employees act harmfully.

On the issue of fairness which Williams raises, any corporation reaps tremendous gain from the actions of the employee, compared to what the employee gains from those same activities. It would not seem to be fair to allow the law to support the profits made by the corporation from the actions of its employees as is done concerning corporate property rights, and yet not penalize the corporation for these same employee actions when they are criminal.[35] Also, there are other fairness-related issues which show that the corporation and its executive officers should be made to pay the penalty for criminal corporate acts.

Some would also claim that the *mens rea* restriction undercuts the application of the theory of vicarious responsibility to the domain of corporations. It might be said that no intent at all is possible for corporate entities since these entities lack minds altogether. But this claim fails to take into account that all aspects of corporate life depend on what real human beings, as members of the corporation, do. The Model Penal Code, recognizing this problem, stated the following principle for the ascription of *mens rea* to corporations. It is necessary for the establishment of *mens rea* for the corporation that

> the commission of the offense was authorized, requested, commanded, performed or recklessly tolerated by the board of directors or by a high managerial agent acting in behalf of the corporation within the scope of his office or employment.[36]

And the authorization must be for that particular act which was criminal rather than merely a blanket authorization which happened to allow for the crime. For in the latter case, it is merely negligent (or perhaps reckless) of the corporation to allow the employee to be in a position to perform this act. And any punishment of the corporation or of high-ranking officers will be based on recklessness or negligence of high-ranking managers, not on the original state of mind of the employee.

The *mens rea* condition will generally mitigate the unfairness of the application of vicarious criminality to corporations. It is a long-standing principle in Anglo-American law that the state of mind of a given person does not transfer to another due to authorization or any other basis of vicarious agency. Hence, while it may be that a corporation can be held responsible for the criminal actions of a given employee, the corporation will not be held to exactly the same degree of liability as the employee could be, unless high-ranking managers have the same state of mind as that employee. As Perkins notes, "Some fault should be required for conviction even if it is no more than failure to exercise a rather high degree of care."[37] It must be remembered that criminal sanctions will be imposed based only on the extent of guilt exhibited by the executives of the corporation. Given this fact, there will be an even greater incentive for executives to try to minimize the extent of criminal penalties by taking every precaution against the possible criminal activities of the corporation's employees. The negligence of the high-ranking managers can establish the *mens rea* of the corporation. The corporation can block the claim that it is criminally responsible by showing that there was no negligence on the part of these high-ranking managers, and thus no criminal state of mind attributable to the corporation.

Hence, it turns out that the major theoretical and moral objections against vicarious corporate responsibility do not constitute sufficient reasons for rejecting this theory. The *actus reus*, like any other act ascribable to the corporation, can be said to transfer to the corporation from the employee, without major theoretical problems. And the *mens rea*, while it does not transfer from the employee, can be found in the states of mind of the supervisors, board members, or executives of the corporation to which the *actus reus* has been transferred.

I turn next to the problem of what sort of punishment or penalty can be justified morally and prudentially when it is found that the corporation is guilty of a crime. Normally the high-ranking members of the corporation will be linked to the criminal act through their negligence. It is my view that sometimes these high-ranking managers, rather than the corporation as a whole, should be criminally sanctioned when the corporation is found to be criminally responsible for a harm.

I argued above that certain members of the corporation, other than those who performed the original act deemed to be criminal, can be linked to the act by their positions of authority and then also by the specific guilty state of mind that each had. Thus, one answer to the problem of punishment of corporations is simply to distribute the punishment among those key members of the corporation who can be so linked to the crime. Two other options involve the penalization of the whole corporation as a unit, either by assessing a penalty against the corporate assets, or by adversely affecting the corporation's image by court-ordered adverse publicity concerning the criminal acts. I will first explain why I think these other two schemes are defective, and then show why similar worries are not applicable to my scheme for assigning punishment in cases of corporate criminality.

First, let us examine briefly the strategy of punishing corporate criminality by penalizing the whole corporation through fines. The reason for employing this strategy is initially quite appealing. If the corporation is indeed itself responsible for the crime, then it makes sense to seek a means of punishment that adversely affects the whole corporation. Yet, this is not as easy as it may appear, for the corporation has few characteristics which could be the object of punishment or penalty. Perhaps the easiest solution to this problem is to try to set a monetary figure corresponding to the normal punishment for the crime in question, and then levy that penalty against that which is most clearly a characteristic of the whole corporation, its assets. This strategy has the consequence of distributing the punishment throughout the entire corporation and thus seemingly comes closest to the model of individual punishment.

But there are many well-known difficulties with this strategy. Most important is the practical fact that many corporations can, and do, pass along to their customers any penalties that are assessed against the corporation. The only remedy for this defect is to force the corporation not to raise its prices, yet that would require quite an intrusive interference in the "free market" operations of businesses and would itself raise many other difficulties. There is also a practical problem with this approach which raises problems of fairness. If the penalty is set too high, the board of directors may declare bankruptcy. Such a response to the attempted punishment is, in effect, like the suicide of a convicted individual criminal but with one major difference — the corporate officers can reform themselves into a "new" corporation (chartered in a different jurisdiction) the very next day. And who is it that is hurt by this strategy of corporate punishment? Normally, only the employees and low-level managers are hurt by corporate bankruptcy. And yet these individuals are not necessarily the ones who have played the greatest causal role or who were the most guilty of the crime in question. Indeed, this strategy generally distributes the punishment to the members of the corporation in such a way as to have no connection with the benefits or roles that these members had in the commission of the crime.

Peter French has recently proposed a variation on the standard strategy for assigning punishment to the entire corporation. French suggests that shame rather than monetary penalty may be a more efficacious strategy in meting out corporate punishment. Specifically, he suggests that "court ordered adverse publicity" be used to shame the corporation, thereby threatening "the offender's prestige and public image" rather than the monetary assets of that corporation.[38] Furthermore, French claims that the way in which this court-ordered adverse publicity will affect the prestige of the offending corporation will be by causing some sort of "identity crisis" within the corporation[39] and by socially stigmatizing the corporation. I wish to raise questions, however, about both the effects on self-image and on public image of the corporation wrought by what French calls "The Hester Prynne Sanction."

French himself points out that this sanction will be effective against the self-image of the person only if the criminal is "concerned with personal worth,"[40] based "on a sensibility to oneself."[41] But in order to have these characteristics, it would seem that the entity in question would have to have a personality. Yet, French has only managed to demonstrate that at best the corporation can be said to have a "mind" in the sense that it has a decision-making structure. Having a decision-making structure is not sufficient for having the kind of personality that would be affected by a concern for personal growth. While it is true that corporations have concern for their self-images, this is not necessarily because of a moral concern for the integrity of the self, but often is merely a public relations worry, that is, a worry about how others will react concerning future profitability. For an entity to truly feel shame as a response to internal rather than external image assessment, that entity must have something like a conscience in which the self comes to worry about its own past conduct and to seek to minimize its own future negative assessments of its conduct, not just to worry about the responses likely to be made by other persons.

Why, it might be asked, can't the corporation be said to reflect conscientiously in a vicarious way through its high-ranking managers? The corporation has a decision-making structure which is, in some sense, distinct from the decision-making structures of the members of the corporation. But the corporation does not have a conscience distinct from the consciences of its members. The corporate decision-making structure is composed of the decision-making structures of management or the board members, which have been blended together into an institutional structure in such a way that a consensus can often be reached about very practical problems which affect the conduct of business of the corporation. But this structure is designed to deal only with business interests. So when the board members or high-ranking managers evaluate the past actions of the corporation it is normally not with a sense of worry about how well or ill the corporation has lived up to a particular moral ideal which is collectively recognized, but rather only in regard to the business aspects of those past actions. Moral concerns which are considered, and which may even be subjected to a vote, are merely the concerns of each conscientious member of the board. For there to be a melding of consciences into an institutionalized superconscience of the corporation, in an analogous way to the manner in which all the individual decision-making structures are blended in the corporation's decision structure, conscientious reflection would have to be goal- or task-oriented. But, such an orientation would not much resemble true conscientious reflection.

In a 1983 article, I argued that conscience is much more closely related to self-interest than is generally acknowledged. So one might think that I would be inclined to support the notion of corporate conscience, since corporations clearly reach decisions concerning their self-interest.[42] But, conscientious reflection does not merely require self-interested calculation, it also involves a concern for one's past actions now assessed in a very odd type of self-interested way, that is, in terms of a regard for the coherence and integrity of that self (what is generally described as the motivation to be in harmony with oneself). This important part of conscience is not goal- or task-oriented since it isn't future-oriented at all. It is this type of reflection that epitomizes conscientious reflection and from which feelings of shame result.

Most significantly, shame is not something which one person can make another person feel. Shame is based on the assessment of past actions in terms of the standards that one has set for oneself. This may be partially influenceable by others, as when one tries to shame another into an act, but the influence must be based on standards of conduct which an individual has already set for himself or herself. Even if a corporation could feel shame in the same way that an individual person could, this personality characteristic could not be created by a court of law unless the corporation was already on the verge of making this assessment on its own. Furthermore, the corporation's decision-making structure is not at all set up for that type of backward-looking personal reflection.

Let us consider one further attempt to save this first part of French's thesis, namely, one which asks why the corporate conscience could not be a high-ranking manager (in the role of a corporate ombudsman)[43] who is delegated the task of morally assessing the past actions of the corporation? Couldn't such a person be shamed; and couldn't his or her shame affect the future conduct of the corporation? Given what I have said about the vicarious way in which corporations think or act, such a possibility cannot be ruled out. For court-ordered shame to be parallel to personal shame, though, it would have to be the case that the ombudsman was on the verge of condemning the past conduct of the corporation in the same way that the court was condemning that conduct. And such a coincidence of judgment could not be guaranteed by any sort of institutionalized office, even that of ombudsman. Yet without this guarantee of coincidence of judgment between judge and jury on the one hand and ombudsman on the other, it could not be guaranteed that the internal reflective assessment of the corporation's behavior by the ombudsman would be negative.

At best, what one can expect to occur in the corporate boardroom is that individual board members come to feel shame for the past acts of the corporation, acts in which they each participated. But conscientious reflection is not likely to be something which is done

by vote or by the deliberations which corporate decision-making structures have been established to produce. The corporation may have
a limited mind, but it has neither the reflective capacities nor the feelings necessary for it to have regard for the past acts it has engaged
in. Thus, the corporation does not have the kind of full-blown personality structure that could conscientiously reflect on itself and feel
shame for what it has done.[44]

The second way that French hopes that his new strategy will
be effective is through the public's reaction to the court-ordered adverse
publicity. Such adverse publicity will indeed have an effect on the
corporation, but shame seems not to be the proper way of understanding what will transpire. Rather, contrary to what French asserts, the
loss in social esteem and the corresponding loss in profitability that
the corporation will face is the only punch behind this policy. This
is mainly due to the consideration above concerning the lack of a
mechanism for feeling shame within the corporation. And yet if it
is the monetary effect, now indirectly realized, of the court action that
is important, then all of the criticisms of monetary penalties imposed
on corporations by courts for criminal activity resurface. Most especially, one would wonder about the fairness of a policy which creates
the same penalty for all members of a corporation when these members
had decidedly different contributions to the criminal result they are
now each being penalized for.

Peter French's strategy, however, may be adapted to become
an alternative to monetary penalties assessed against high-ranking
managers of a corporation in cases where the corporation is held guilty
of corporate crimes. Those who believe that jail is not a fair punishment for people who have not directly caused a crime may feel that
court-ordered adverse publicity of the high-ranking manager's deeds
will sufficiently stigmatize the manager in future business dealings
to constitute adequate punishment. Since the individual board member
or high-ranking manager of the corporation is a person with a full
personality, and hence with a sense of self-esteem, such a shame-based
strategy will be more likely to be effective.

I favor, though, the more standard criminal sanctions brought
against those key individuals who have participated in a corporate
criminal act. Such a strategy has several distinct advantages over the
other two strategies. First, it does not unfairly treat the individuals
involved since a premium is placed on letting the degree of individual

punishment fit the degree of individual guilt. But also those who have not benefitted significantly from the crime will not be those who are the people most adversely affected by the punishment. The organizational chart will identify the members of the corporation who stand most to gain by the crime and they can then be linked to the *actus reus*. Yet, the type of corporate criminal punishment I propose is not based on strict liability. Rather, being guilty is still an essential ingredient in the determination of who is to be punished and to what extent these persons will be punished for the crime. While lower-level employees also may be punished when their guilt has been established, high-ranking managers will become the main focus of litigation, given their employer-like status in the corporation.

Second, the fear of personal punishment will weigh much more heavily on the minds of these corporate officers than would the other strategies. This will make it more likely that they will prevent future harms. Since it is not possible to pass along their punishment to the customers, as was done with the penalties of the first strategy, much more caution will be taken. Most importantly, the practice of factoring in the potential costs of adverse legal rulings when decisions are being made about what products to put on the market, will be diminished. For few people will risk personal liberty for increased corporate profits.

The strategy of holding individual members (especially high-ranking members) of the corporation responsible for the crimes committed in corporate settings has the major advantage of allowing the criminal justice system to operate in the manner in which it has proven successful: dealing with personal involvement in the commission of crimes. If an act is judged to be a crime, society takes the matter seriously, indeed sometimes so seriously that it deprives the perpetrator of his or her liberty. If members of a gang conspire to engage in activities that run a high risk of injuring or killing innocent bystanders, those individuals are subject to the loss of liberty which jail sentences embody and the person who planned the crime is often given the stiffest sentence. When members of a corporation engage in conduct with similar risks, the societal response should also be similar.

If an individual employer puts his or her employees into a position where harm is likely to occur, and doesn't properly supervise them, the employer is held, at a minimum, to be criminally negligent. When the employees are members of a corporation, then the supervisor and other high-ranking members of the corporation who authorized their conduct should be treated similarly to the individual employer. And the rationale in both cases is the same: harmful conduct should be punished, inside as well as outside of the corporate sector. If corporate officers come to recognize that they are likely to be held criminally negligent in such cases, they will come to exercise more caution over those acts they can influence, and harmful conduct will surely be diminished. This is the proper, perhaps the only proper, goal of the criminal law. As the Supreme Court recognized in *U.S.* v. *Park*, it is justified to use criminal "sanctions which reach and touch the individuals who execute the corporate mission."[45]

IV. Distributing Responsibility in Mobs

In section I of this current chapter, I claimed that collective responsibility could be attributed to a mob when there were both actions and intentions in the mob that were caused, at least in part, by the structure of the mob. In this section I will talk about the way that responsibility should be distributed once it is found that a mob or other unorganized group is collectively responsible for a given result. Finally, I will build on the previously developed analogy between conspiracies and corporate criminality to address the difficult question of distributing blame and punishment throughout social groups such as mobs.

A given amateur sports team member may not contribute much to a given victory and yet it nonetheless can be said that the entire team was responsible for the victory. This result can be explained by noting that the member did play some role (by being ready to replace one of the starters, for example) even if not a direct role. In one sense, Feinberg may be right to say that the condition of contributory fault (or guilt) is "weakened" in collective responsibility,[46] that is, not every member must be at fault to the same extent in order for collective responsibility to be assigned. But since the ascription of collective responsibility does not mean that the individual member is yet held individually responsible, it is not the case that a significant weakening of the fault condition has occurred. The group still needs to be contributing to the harm in a faulty (or guilty) way in order for the harm to be correctly said to be the responsibility of a group such as a mob. Problems arise, if at all, only when an attempt is made to distribute the responsibility among the members at some later date.

Virginia Held has argued that there are two distinct types of group entities: those which have a collective decision procedure and those which do not (all groups in this latter category she calls "random"). She contends that when a group has a decision procedure, then responsibility ascriptions to the group will not result in responsibility ascriptions to each of the members of the group as individuals. But when there is no decision procedure, then the responsibility of the group distributes to the members of the group.[47] Held allows that the degree of responsibility may vary for each of these members, but this is said to be only of minor importance in the moral domain.

Held has also claimed that "in saying that the moral responsibility of a random collection is distributive, we may not be saying very much; for if the action is one that could be taken by the random collection only as a group, questions about apportioning responsibility for various components of the action, assuming that the action can be broken down into its components, remains open."[48] As one might glean from these remarks, Held believes that ascriptions of responsibility to an unorganized group are very important and not mere shorthand reformulations of what is going on morally with each member of the group. Held seems to take seriously the capacity for joint action by groups which do not have formal, explicit decision procedures, even as she claims that having that decision procedure is of great importance for the ability of the group to act in a concerted fashion.

Most importantly, Held argues that the members of an unorganized group may be said to be responsible for not taking an action that could have prevented a harm from occurring. She considers the case of Kitty Genovese, whose neighbors all failed to telephone for help as Ms. Genovese lay bleeding to death outside of her apartment building. Any of these neighbors could have taken steps to prevent serious harm to Ms. Genovese, yet none did. The group as a whole is responsible and so is each member of that group. Similarly, she argues that the passengers on a subway train can be said to be responsible for not aiding a child who is attacked and beaten by older youths in front of these passengers. In this case, the members should have formed themselves into an organized group to use their concerted strength to prevent the harm from occurring. Here, unlike the Geno-

vese case, each person is not responsible for the whole harm, since
no one person could have single-handedly prevented it from occurring. But each person is responsible for not doing what each could
have done. According to Held, in an unorganized group each person is responsible for the component part or role which that person's
action or inaction served in a given result.

While I wish to arrive at conclusions similar to Held about the
ascription of collective responsibility to unorganized groups, I feel
that she and others have placed too much emphasis on the formal
decision procedure as a chief condition for distinguishing types of
groups and hence also in determining collective responsibility. Stanley
Bates in criticizing Held points out that formal decision procedures
do not exhaust the category of "group decision methods," and hence
some collections of persons may be able to reach group decisions even
though no formal procedure exists by which this is accomplished.[49]
Unfortunately, Bates did not pursue this issue in his critique of Held.
Held's analysis has trouble with mobs because she fails to see that
groups can be unified but not organized.

If, as was argued in the previous chapter, mobs and other unorganized groups can be said to have sufficient unity to manifest a
kind of intentional conduct, then responsibility ascriptions which are
not fully distributive can be made to these social groups even though
they lack decision procedures. In this final section of chapter four,
I wish to discuss possible ways of distributing responsibility for the
harmful consequences of mob actions. Clearly, if the preceding analysis
is correct, no easy translation of mob responsibility into the responsibility of mob members is possible; for the responsibility ascribed
to the group is not merely the aggregation of responsibilities of the
members of the group. But, as was true in the case of corporate
criminality, this does not mean that there is no possible ascription
of individual responsibility on the basis of collective responsibility.

In light of the analysis of corporate criminality, we might look
for a leader of the mob, or at least someone who played a key role
in causally constituting the mob. Such a person, like the president
of a corporation, plays a more significant role in the actions of the
group than does a mere member. The one who leads or constitutes
a social group is usually more responsible for the harmful consequences
of that group's action than are the other members. The formation
of the group added a capacity for action that goes beyond what in-

dividuals acting on their own are capable of. This capacity would not have been added if it were not for the actions of this key figure in the group's history. In what follows, I will argue that those who play key causal roles in the actions of groups, even those in groups which are unorganized, are more responsible than those who do not play these key roles.

Think for a moment of the harmful actions taken by an audience in a crowded movie theater when one member of that crowd yells "Fire!" The behavior of the other members of the audience is virtually automatic. These members have been started in motion by the yeller, who has successfully panicked each person with quite predictable results. It seems reasonable to say that this person has a special responsibility for the harmful result. Indeed, in this case, the yeller may be the only person who can be said to have individual responsibility for what has occurred.

The reason for ascribing responsibility to the yeller is that the yeller has played a causally significant role in turning the members of the audience into a panic-stricken crowd. But for the actions of the yeller, the crowd would not have been formed into a group which, for example, could trample the usher under foot. Of course, causal responsibility does not always translate into individual moral responsibility. But when the results are so easily predictable, it may be possible to move from causal to individual moral responsibility.

It is inappropriate to hold the members of the stampeding audience responsible for the harm to the usher since these people could not have acted otherwise than the way they were compelled to act by sheer panic.[50] Only one person in the audience, the yeller, could have acted otherwise, and this person is also the one who plays a conscious causal role in bringing about the harm. If there are members of mobs who also play such a conscious causal role in the mob's behavior, then a similar argument can be advanced to show that these individual persons, above all other members, should be singled out for special responsibility for the consequences of the mob's behavior.

This way of assigning individual responsibility for those harms which are deemed to be the result of collective action is similar to the way that Held suggests. The role played by a given member becomes crucial in assigning blame or punishment to that person. But unlike Held, I believe that the key members of unorganized groups may sometimes be the only ones who are individually responsible for

such harms as those that result from mob violence. Like the key
members of formally organized groups, one should look to those who
are individually responsible, and this is not just because it is difficult
to identify the components of a mob's action. It may be because a
large number of the members were not aware of intending to play
the roles they did play in the end result. But if, instead, the members
of a mob resemble conspirators in that each member joined the group
intending to bring about a joint undertaking, then I would follow Held
in thinking that each member can be held responsible for her or his
part in that joint undertaking.

Joseph Ellin has argued against this view that as long as the
members of a group had a common criminal purpose in joining a
given group, it does not matter what each member did to bring about
a given result. "Each individual is at fault for joining the conspiracy,
for accepting its unlawful purpose, and for entering into a course of
action which may result in actions by others over whom he has no
control."[51] I agree that a member of a given group is always responsible for entering the group. But even if the group is constituted for
illegal purposes, this does not mean that each member intends that
these illegal purposes be carried out. If each person who joins such
a group did intend all of the illegal purposes of the group, then I would
support Ellin in his claims. But, at least in the cases of mob action
we have been considering, joining a group is not the same as reflectively accepting all of the purposes of the group. There are many social
groups which cannot be treated as conspiracies, and mobs, as well
as certain associations, often cannot be so treated since certain key
members of the group may cause the group to pursue purposes which
no other member of the group reflectively intended to pursue.

Should the key members of mobs be held responsible for all the
harm that results from a mob's action? I think not. Rather, the share
in the blame or punishment borne by the key members should be
greater than it is for the other members of the group. This may mean
that some of the harm caused by a given group is not the individual
responsibility of any member of that group, and this is precisely why
I have claimed throughout that collective responsibility is not a form
of distributive responsibility. Only in those cases where individuals
are causally responsible and at fault (or guilty) for the existence of
the structure can the blame be fully distributed to individuals. But
many cases do not seem to be of this sort.

As with the examples of corporate criminality discussed above, in distributing individual responsibility it is helpful to be able to say that a person's group has already been shown to be collectively responsible for a given harmful result. The prosecution or blame of individual leaders of a mob is difficult since these individuals might not directly cause any of the harms in question. Just as was true for the person who yelled "Fire" in a theater, the harm may be caused by someone else — the members who are not necessarily the leaders — and yet these people often lack the requisite intent to be considered guilty or blameworthy. But if the group itself is collectively responsible for a harmful result, and a given individual is found to have been a leader of that group, then it is not inappropriate to hold him or her individually responsible for at least part of the harm. As with corporate presidents, mob leaders may be found criminally responsible for the harms caused by their groups.

5. Common Interests and Group Rights

The first four chapters form a unit in which the central concern is with the ethical analysis of the purposive joint actions of social groups. The next three chapters also form a unit the core of which is the ethical analysis of the common interests and rights of social groups. The capacity for having interests is a weaker condition than the capacity to engage in purposive action — but, as I will argue, it is nonetheless a sufficient condition for the ascription of such moral concepts as rights and harms. I explore these subjects in the next two chapters. Then, in the final chapter, I will conclude my study with a discussion of some political and legal strategies which have been proposed to redress violation of rights and other harms to social groups.

The first section of this chapter presents a preliminary analysis of the concept of common interest and explains how the interests of ethnic groups, such as Blacks in South Africa, should be conceptualized. The second section briefly outlines my position on common interest in formally organized groups such as corporations, with special emphasis on the way that the corporate interest in free speech should be conceptualized. Corporations are capable of having interests and rights but only in a very restricted way compared to that of rationally mature human individuals. In the third section, the concept of corporate interest is applied to corporate rights to property, comparing these rights to the property rights of individual human beings.

I. The Common Interests of Ethnic Groups

Harm is generally defined as the infringement of an interest. When harm can be substantiated, then the entity which is harmed is thought to have a basis for making claims upon society or individual human beings for the redress or suspension of the harmful practices. In this section I will contend that some social groups can be harmed by the infringement of the common interests of their members. In so arguing, I will provide quite a different basis for ascribing moral predicates to social groups than is normally advanced in philosophical literature. Normally it is thought that only groups which have decision-making procedures can be harmed since only groups of this sort have sufficient cohesion. But given that having an interest does not require complex organizational structure, decision-making procedures, or even the capacity for action, it will turn out that a wide range of social groups can be harmed, and should be recognized as having at least some form of standing to make legitimate moral or legal claims.

I will begin by analyzing the concept of common interest so as to make sense of what Joel Feinberg has called the "vicarious harms" of the members of certain social groups. I will then show that common interest provides the possibility for two distinct types of indirect harm to the members of a group who are not directly harmed by a given practice. I will argue that these interests and harms can be sufficiently group-based to warrant the claim that the social group has moral interests and has moral standing. Finally, I will briefly indicate some of the practical implications of holding that social groups can have moral or legal standing by looking at the case of apartheid in South Africa.

Feinberg has provided an analysis of the most obvious case of common interest. If you are my sole support, then you and I both have a common interest in your well-being. I have such an interest because my own well-being is intimately linked to yours, and hence I am vicariously interested in your own well-being.[1] There is another kind of case, also identified by Feinberg: some people may have an abiding interest in the welfare of other people, seeing the interests of others as "an end in itself."[2] This type of common interest is generally not completely independent of the self-interests of the people involved, since one person's interest in another's welfare normally arises when they are both members of a group which is strongly interdependent. It is for this reason that Feinberg says that the distinction between the two types of case is "somewhat artificial."[3]

Feinberg elsewhere identified this second kind of common interest as being based on a felt solidarity for one's fellow members of a social group. He narrowly focused the discussion on only those groups where there is risk of common failure for joint undertakings, and he thereby recognized that large, diverse groups are generally excluded from having common interests.[4] In contrast I argue that a social group can suffer harm which is not based on a failure of joint undertaking, but which is based on, for instance, mistreatment due to being adversely stereotyped.[5] Such harm can affect large groups of persons who do not necessarily have the capacity to engage in joint undertakings. To understand this criticism of Feinberg, the concepts of common interest and vicarious harm must be more closely analyzed.

To have a moral interest is generally to be in a position justifiably to assert a claim to X. Such claims are justified when the object of the claim is something which is a good for that person, and something which that person wants. Interests are common when the set of wants of all members of a group includes or would include X. If it is legitimate for these people to want X, then they or a representative may stand justified in making joint or collective claims to X, in addition to the individual claims that each may make.

Feinberg is right to think that interests normally concern things that people want to do, such as to engage in free speech. But this does not mean, by analogy, that only those groups of people who want to engage in collective action can have common interests. In addition, groups of people who can be acted upon may also have common interests, even though there is so little organizational structure to the group that the members could not act in concert to protect their interests, or even to issue complaints when their interests are infringed. Ethnic and minority groups are the best examples of groups which may not have the capacity to act but which may nonetheless have interests. Their members can be harmed by the the actions of others, oppressor groups for instance, regardless of whether the ethnic group is organized sufficiently to respond to the harm in common voice or deed. The Black majority in South Africa currently lacks the organizational structure to be able to take effective action against the policy of apartheid foisted upon it by the white government. But this is not relevant in determining whether the group of Blacks in South Africa has interests which are harmed by the policies of apartheid.

What is relevant for determining whether such a group has interests is whether the treatment of members of the group is based on their group membership. And for this to be the case, there must be strong relationships existing among the members of the group, or strong identification of individual persons as group members by external observers. There must be a strong coherence to the group, either in the eyes of the group members themselves or in the eyes of the oppressor group, since without this coherence the harms to some members are not likely also to result in harms to all other members. Later I will explain this in terms of the harmed status of the group. Suffice it here to note that group or collective interest requires that there must be enough coherence to the group for the social group to be said to have an identifiable status.

In a group which has strong coherence, harm of some members also harms all group members. Of course direct harm results to any members who are the primary objects of harmful treatment. Indirect harm results to members of a group, when directly harmful treatment of some members could just as easily have been directed at those who were not directly affected, or when there is strong empathy by other members for those who are directly harmed. In both cases there is an indirect or vicarious harm to the rest of the members when one member is directly harmed.

The type of indirect or vicarious harm which Feinberg and others seem to have missed is that harm occuring to some members of a group when other members of the group are directly harmed simply because of their group membership. If people are in a state of solidarity, in which they identify the interests of others as their own intersts, then most obviously, as Feinberg argues, vicarious harm is possible. But indirect harm can also occur to some members of a group when other members are directly harmed not just as individuals but because they are members of a given group. The individuals not directly affected can be said to be indirectly or vicariously harmed in that their status is adversely affected by what has occurred to their fellow members. Either solidarity characterizes the feelings of the members toward each other, thereby creating empathetic reactions of all to the harm of some members, or indiscriminate treatment of individual persons as group members by outsiders creates a risk of similar treatment of all members of a group.

Solidarity, on the one hand, and common external identification by others, on the other hand, create the kind of interests for group members which warrants giving their groups the standing which allows for justified complaints and claims for redress of harm. The harm suffered by the members of these groups is indeed group-based, and hence not reducible to the aggregate harms and claims of the individual members of these groups.

Harms are group-based when there is something about the structure, or perceived structure, of a given group that makes all of the members of the group at least indirectly or vicariously harmed whenever one of the members is directly harmed. To say that a concept is group-based generally is to say that the full explanation of a given event cannot be made without some reference to a social group or to one of the features of a social group, such as its structure or the relationships among members which characterize the group. For this point to be fully understood, an example is in order.

Think again of the policies of apartheid in South Africa. Some of these policies do not directly affect all Blacks, but only some Blacks. There are international travel restrictions, for instance, which directly affect only those few Blacks wealthy enough to engage in international travel. Perhaps, there are moderately well-off Blacks who would not choose to travel even if apartheid were not in place. How can the direct harm to these few Blacks be group-based? In what sense are all South African Blacks at least indirectly or vicariously harmed by the policies of apartheid?

The discriminatory policies of apartheid are not directed at individual people who happen merely to be Black and hence cannot be explained by reference to the interests of isolated individuals. Rather apartheid is directed at people because they are Black, and only because they are Black, that is because of membership in the Negroid racial group. Whatever features are constitutive of the identities of specific Blacks are irrelevant for the policy of apartheid. Only a person's blackness counts. And since apartheid does not discriminate among individual Black persons, instead treating their blackness as the only characteristic which is normatively important, each Black person is reduced to a mere token of the type "being Black." There is no other morally significant type of which any given Black person is thought to be a token. Explanations of apartheid must make reference to this social factor, and in this sense apartheid needs to be conceived as a group-based harm.

Each person who is a member of an identifiable group has a common interest in not having adverse treatment pegged to group membership. It is a matter of mere coincidence that one Black is harmed and another Black not harmed by a policy which treats Blacks indiscriminately. People and groups who engage in the policy of apartheid are the ones who help perpetuate the rigorous classification of Blacks and who provide that class with a common interest. Various members of the group of Blacks may have no conscious awareness of the identity and interests of the group, and yet it is still true that they are members and that they have common interests with the rest of the members. And most importantly, since this type of common interest is based on adverse treatment of individuals, not as individuals but as members of a given group, it is appropriate to say that the common interest and the harm resulting from the deprivation of that interest are group-based.

It might be thought that more is needed to warrant treating a group as if it had moral standing than merely showing that there are interests and harms that are group-based. However, such is not the case. Showing that there are group-based harms is a way of showing that more is going on than can be captured by the aggregating of harms to individuals who merely happen, for instance, to be Black. It is also a way of showing that the interests of the members of a given group are intertwined with the status of the group. Until the status of the group is changed, the individual members will continue to face the infringement of their common interests, resulting in at least indirect or vicarious harms to all of the members of that group.

A group should be treated as having interests when summing the individual interests of the members of the group does not capture the nature of the common interest, and when some reference to the group (its membership criteria, its structure, etc.) must be made to fully explain the interests of the members. The necessity of making reference to membership criteria warrants talk of common interests as collective or group-based. It is not just that each person is treated on the basis of his or her blackness, but also that all people who display blackness are treated as a coherent group. It is this latter fact which allows interest, and moral standing, to be ascribed to the group. This conceptual point has practical moral consequences as I will next argue.

Moral standing, like legal standing, grants to a given entity the possibility of legitimate claiming. Owen Fiss has argued that social groups, as well as individual human persons, can have legal standing. Fiss is motivated by a belief that bureaucratic organizations increasingly contribute to the deprivation of rights of members of already disadvantaged social groups. Since these organizations, both private corporations and governmental agencies, already have legal standing, he believes that the law will only be able effectively to curb harmful organizational practices if the groups which are harmed by these organizations also having standing to sue.[6]

But Fiss argues for the legal standing of social groups by setting too stringent a set of conditions upon what counts as a social group. Fiss claims, first, that a social group must be an entity with an existence and identity distinct from the members of the group.[7] As I argued in chapter one, this is too strong a requirement. For purposes of the current discussion, Fiss's second condition is the most relevant. He says that there must be interdependence between a group and its members. This means that the members "of the group identify themselves — explain who they are — by reference to their membership in the group," and that the well-being and status of the members of the group "is in part determined by the well-being or status of the group," and vice versa.[8] What I have been arguing is that such an interdependency condition is sufficient for ascribing moral standing to a social group. But, unlike Fiss, I do not hold that it is necessary for the members of a group actually to identify themselves by reference to their group membership, in order for moral standing to be ascribed to the group. It can also be sufficient for moral standing that others treat these members indiscriminately.

Fiss provides an interesting account of how the legal landscape would change if social groups were given standing. For instance, in a society which engaged in differential treatment based on group membership, most political and legal questions concerning racial and sexual discrimination would be addressed in terms of the relative status of the groups. It is the status of a social group, as compared with other social groups in a given society, that would count. Fiss claims that[9]

> blacks are very badly off, probably our worst-off class (in terms of material well-being second only to the American Indians), and in addition they have occupied the lowest rung for several centuries. In a sense they are America's perpetual underclass. It is both of these characteristics — the relative position of the group and the duration of the position — that make efforts to improve the status of the group defensible.[9]

Fiss seeks to justify group-oriented lawsuits often employed in civil rights litigation. In these cases, the direct and indirect harm a social group has suffered is intensified when its relative status can be shown to be low to begin with.[10]

In the case of apartheid in South Africa, a case can also be constructed for group-oriented political or legal efforts aimed at the status of the group made up of Blacks, not just at the specific economic or political problems of isolated Blacks. But such a case is thought to raise a significant problem. There seems to be a conflict between those individual Blacks who are the beneficiaries of apartheid, and those who would urge political action to aid the group of Blacks by overthrowing apartheid.

This question raises the problem of conflicts between individuals and groups which are given moral standing, as well as the problem of conflicts among groups. These problems will be taken up in greater detail in the final chapter on justice, but suffice it to say that applying the concept of indirect harm to the individual members of groups that are invidiously discriminated against allows one to see that the group-based harms are often as real as harms to those few Black individuals who benefit from discriminatory policies such as apartheid. More importantly, incremental strategies will not be effective at remedying such problems, especially when the indiscriminate treatment of Blacks is entrenched within a governmental bureaucracy and supported by state sanctions. Any individual harm incurred in the attempt to dismantle apartheid must be weighed against the severe harm suffered by the members of the group, and by the difficulty of redressing the harms suffered by the members of the group in any other way.[11]

Questions concerning conflicts among groups must be addressed as comparative status questions. It might be argued that the white minority in South Africa is also the kind of group that has collective interests and which should be given moral or legal standing. Of course, the previous discussion has set the stage for such an assertion. But notice that the status of the white minority in South Africa is anything but disadvantaged. Indeed, their interests have been enhanced rather than harmed, to the detriment of the interests of Blacks, for so long that there cannot be much moral suasion to any claims these whites might make as a group. If white South Africans are also a social group with common interests, then they also should have moral standing. But they must still document harms to their group in order to be justified in exercising their standing to make claims. The likelihood that these claims could be justified should not be dismissed. But given the history of the region, such a likelihood should not diminish the importance of the claims for the redress of the easily documented harms to Blacks.

In conclusion, I have tried throughout this section to show that a much wider range of social groups should be afforded moral standing than is normally accepted in contemporary ethics.[12] The focus has been on groups which are not highly organized but which nonetheless have the capacity to have interests and to be harmed. In some cases it is legitimate to say that these interests and harms are sufficiently collective or group-based to warrant granting moral or legal standing to the group. Such a conceptual scheme has important practical implications, especially in the case of the harms generated by the policies of apartheid against Blacks in South Africa.

II. Corporate Interests

If ethnic and minority groups should have moral and legal standing because they can be harmed, it seems uncontroversial that corporations and other highly organized groups should have this moral and legal standing as well. But do corporations have more than this passive basis for having rights? Corporations have interests based on their ability to be harmed, but they also have interests based on their ability to engage in joint action. Do these other interests of the corporation provide a basis for corporate rights of the sort that individual human persons have as a result of their action-based interests? I will argue that corporate interests are not similar to the interests of individual persons. As a result, it often happens that the rights afforded to individual humans should not be afforded, at least without restrictions, to corporations. This section begins to explore the relationship between interests and rights for social groups. In the next section (section III) I will develop the analysis of corporate interests and rights with an extended example, a conceptual analysis of corporate property rights.

In our culture, various legal rights are enforced for human beings because of our shared belief that human beings have an interest in the enforcement of those rights. These interests derive from our natures, our needs, and the social conditions necessary to ensure that we have opportunities to act to fulfill our needs. Certain interests, for example, are of special importance in regard to the rights to free expression. These are the interests in autonomy and in true and informed belief. If corporations indeed merit the legal protection of their expressions just as individual humans do, then these rights should be based on the corporate counterpart of the individual human interests in autonomy and in true and informed belief.[13] To determine whether or not there are such common interests, we must first consider which kinds of action-based interests corporations can have.

A corporation comprises a plurality of individuals, each a moral agent in her or his own right, who are now associated in a joint venture, and who form a decision-making procedure to aid in this venture. In the case of for-profit corporations, the joint venture is aimed at economic profit-making. Because the corporation has goals and interests that are the result of interactions within the corporation, it has seemed to some theorists that incorporation brings into being a whole new entity, "a corporate person," whose actions have a moral and legal status all its own. For such theorists, corporations can have interests and assert rights claims based on their ability to act, in just the same way as individual human beings can.

In contrast to this, other theorists solve the ontological puzzle of the corporation by construing it as nothing more than the sum of its constituent individuals, and, therefore, not as an agent or rights-bearer which is in any way distinct from those constituent individuals. Along the continuum between these extremes lies a whole range of possible intermediate positions. Each of these positions has implications for the ascription of such rights as free speech or property to corporations.

Peter French is well known for advocating the view at one end of the corporate ontology continuum, that the corporation is a full moral person in its own right. French regards corporations as "members of the moral community, of equal status with the traditionally acknowledged residents: biological human beings."[14] Within this framework, the actions of the corporation members constitute the intentional actions of the corporation when they have what French calls a "procedurally corporate aspect" and when these actions instantiate or implement "established corporate policy".[15]

If the corporation is a moral person of "equal standing" with individual human beings, then corporations would have the same array of moral and legal rights as human beings. Are there common interests within the corporation equivalent to individual human interests in autonomy or in true and informed belief, which could be the basis for a moral right, for instance, to the legal protection of expression? French regards corporations as having "interests in doing those things that are likely to result in realization of their established corporate goals."[16] Although he considers corporate interests to be more stable and less wide-ranging than the interests of individual human beings, he sees no other significant differences between them.

For a corporation to have an "interest" in the realization of its economic goals and activities similar to the interests of individual human persons in their goals and activities, it must have the capacity to be interested. But corporate action is, in one important sense, dependent upon the actions of individual human beings who are interrelated in various ways. Hence, it is tempting to reject French's view altogether and to consider the corporation's interests in realizing its goals to be merely a *summation* of the interests of the current, and perhaps past, employees, managers, and stockholders of the corporation. For the corporation's interests to be more than this, as French would have it, there must be some way that the corporation itself can be actively interested which is recognizably *of* the corporation itself and not a mere aggregation of the interests of its members. While the corporation can make decisions through its decision-making procedures, nothing in the corporation is active independently of the individuals who constitute the corporation. So there isn't anything within the corporation which is itself actively interested or which generates interests because of its activities. Of course, it may be that there are interests imposed on the corporation, or that there are common interests arising out of the strong feelings the members have for each other, as was the case with ethnic and minority groups. But these interests are not sufficiently like human action-based interests to warrant claiming that the corporation should be understood as having the same interests and rights as individual human persons.

The primary limitation on corporate interests is that the corporation is not *embodied* and *active* in the world in a form which is separate or distinct from the embodiments and actions of its constituent members. Ontologically speaking, its only realization in the world is by means of embodiment in its individually separate members and their individual actions. The corporation is *inherently* a composite being, constructed out of a plurality of beings each of whom is already a whole and coherent moral person in her or his own right. A human individual, by contrast, is *not* a being whose only realization in the world is constituted out of a collection of beings each of which is a whole and coherent person.

When a human individual acts, it is she or he as a whole person, who acts; when a human individual has interests, it is she as a whole person, and not any of her constituent parts, which has interests. By contrast, when a corporation acts or has interests, the realization of these actions or these interests is *only* possible by means of the actions or interests of its constituent members, that is, through individual human action and interest. The corporation is inherently a complex entity whose actions and interests depend essentially upon what are already coherent *personal* acts and interests at a noncorporate level of analysis. In chapter two, this ontologically derivative status of corporate action is referred to as manifesting "vicarious agency."[17] The corporation indeed acts, as French argues, but unlike human beings, the corporation can act only *vicariously*, through the actions of its members following designated procedures. Analogously, I now argue, a corporation only has *interests* vicariously. Thus, I reject French's view that the corporation has interests and rights equivalent to individual human beings. Hence, this eliminates one possible basis for arguing that corporations have moral rights of free expression and property normally afforded to individual humans.

French's view of the interests and rights of the corporation lies at one end of a continuum of viewpoints; at the other lies extreme individualism, in particular, the view that corporate rights are nothing more than the rights of the members of corporations. A representative theorist of this view of corporate rights is Roger Pilon.[18] He contends that the corporation should be seen as having "whatever rights and obligations its owners *have* to exercise through it, *can* exercise through it, and have stipulated in their articles of incorporation *are to be* exercised through it."[19] His position reduces corporate interests and rights completely to the interests and rights of the individual persons who own the corporation, that is, the shareholders. Concerning the interest in, and right to, free speech, Pilon claims that corporations have such interests and rights precisely to the same extent that their owners have these rights as individual human persons.[20] The corporation *per se* does not have rights at all, on Pilon's view; nonetheless, by transfer of rights and by contract, its owners create something which may be *regarded* as rights for the corporation, but which is really an aggregate of individual rights.

One obvious problem with Pilon's view is that the current owners of the corporation do not operate legally as a mere aggregate of individuals who happen to be doing business together. Limited liability for torts is something which they each acquire in virtue of the special status of incorporation and it is something which they would *not* have if they were merely doing business together as individuals. I will defend this position in the next section of the current chapter. Suffice it to say that a strict individualism gives us an inadequate analysis of corporate interest. The individual interests of the corporation must often be defined in terms which presuppose incorporation with others in a joint venture. Also presupposed are a charter and decision-making procedure as a shared framework within which various individual interests are coordinated. It is this point which makes me part company with strict individualism.

While there are problems with French's collectivist view of corporate interests and rights, and with regarding the corporation as a moral person *fully* equivalent to a human being, I am more sympathetic to his modified collectivism than to Pilon's extreme individualism. The corporation is capable of decisions, actions, interests, and rights — but only *vicariously* so. That is, it *is* legitimate to construe certain individual interests, especially those expressed in and consistent with the corporate charter and other policy statements, as being the (collective) interests of the corporation. But it must not be forgotten that these interests, and the policy statements with which they are consistent, are all, at an important level of analysis, the interests and doings of beings who are already, in their own right, individual moral persons.

The correct ontological conclusion to draw is that corporations are the sorts of entities which can have action-based interests, but only vicariously. Thus, their moral standing is of a narrower sort than that of individual human beings. Also, the interest which corporations are capable of having in such rights as that of free expression will be circumscribed by the same limitations which define the corporate nature in general. The specific argument showing that there should not be the same legal protection of corporate rights as for individual human rights will be given in chapter six, section I.

So far I have argued that the corporation's interests are narrower and more restricted than are individual human interests. So, too, the corporation should have moral standing of a much diminished sort as compared to individual human beings. In the next section I will analyze the rights to property often attributed to corporations as a way of further refining the idea of corporate interest.

III. Corporate Property Rights

This section will expand the previous discussion of corporate interests and rights through an extended conceptual analysis of corporate property rights. I will first argue that corporate property rights cannot be fully explained by reference to the aggregate rights of stockholders, or even the aggregate rights of stockholders plus managers. I then set out an analysis of corporate property rights which takes into account the disanalogies that exist between corporate and individual rights. I conclude by arguing that legal and political policy should not afford corporate property rights an equivalent status to that of individual property rights.

According to legal theory in most western societies, stockholders own the corporation, while the corporation can own land and other assets in its own name. It thus seems reasonable to think that individual stockholders are the ultimate owners of the property held in the corporation's name. If corporate property could be so easily reduced to individual property claims of stockholders, then there would be no special problems in moral or legal theory posed by corporate property rights. But there are good reasons for questioning this simple reduction. While it is true that legally stockholders own the corporate property, they do so collectively, not individually. No one stockholder owns all of any particular corporate asset. (By "stockholder" I mean someone who owns an individual share of stock in a given company or corporation.) Thus, no stockholder can unilaterally stipulate the uses of these assets. And even while it may be true that the stockholders collectively own the corporation; it is not necessarily true that they have full ownership in the sense of having the kind of control over the corporate assets that ordinary, individual property owners have.[21]

Since Roman times it has been thought that the right to a thing was a function of ownership and control of a given thing. In today's corporations, even the aggregate of stockholders do not exercise full control over the use (or abuse) of corporate assets. (By "full control" I mean what the classical political economists meant by saying that an individual was at liberty to do precisely what he or she chose with the thing to which one had a right, as long as no one was harmed.) Managerial prerogative complicates any discussion of corporate property rights. In practice, stockholders do not exercise direct control over the use of corporate assets. Instead, the stockholders merely affirm or veto specific recommendations made by management.[22] Seemingly, stockholders do not have the full control over the use of a thing which was the hallmark of individual property rights. Berle and Means claim that there were three functions connected together in the concept of private property,

> that of having interests in an enterprise, that of having power over it, and that of acting with respect to it. . . . Before the industrial revolution, the owner-worker performed all three, as do most farmers today. But during the nineteenth century the bulk of industrial production came to be carried out by enterprises in which a division had occurred, the owner fulfilling the first two functions, while the latter was in large measure performed by a separate group, the hired managers.[23]

And with the rise of the modern corporation in the twentieth century, having an interest in and having power over were also separated from each other. The conclusion seems inescapable:

> In examining the breakup of the old concept that was property and the old unity that was private enterprise, it is therefore evident that we are dealing not only with distinct but often with opposing groups.[24]

It might be claimed, though that there has been an explicit or implicit relinquishing of control over these corporate assets on the part of the stockholders and that without the relinquishing of this control managers would have no prerogative at all. Hence this would reestablish the contention that stockholders still own the corporate property. I believe that there are two reasons for thinking that stockholders have not merely relinquished their control in this manner. First, most large corporations have such an intricate decision-making structure that an individual stockholder would find it difficult to initiate or enforce a given policy even if the stockholder should desire such an opportunity. Second, and more important, stockholders do not have the right to exercise control unless they combine together to form at least a majority of all of the stockholders. There is a significant difference between owning a thing and owning a share of a thing. When one owns a share, one's control is limited by the fact that one must receive support from other share-owners in order effectively to exercise one's control. But even securing cooperation from a majority of one's fellow share-owners does not necessarily result in control. The legal policy concerning corporate control allows managers to govern, even over the objections of a majority of stockholders.[25]

This last consideration shows that even when stockholders can find a majority of fellow members in support of a given policy, they do not necessarily end up with control over the policy-making decisions concerning the use of corporate assets. But even without this consideration, individual stockholders exercise very little control over corporate policy on their own. Minority stockholders do not even have the right to place any of their own representatives on the corporate board of directors in most states, although this may be changing as some states adopt more democratic voting policies for directors.[26]

If ownership is properly ascribed to those who control a thing, then managers have a claim to ownership of the corporate assets. But if entitlement is the basis of ownership, then stockholders have a much greater claim than do managers. If, as seems most reasonable, ownership should be ascribed to those who control and are entitled to benefit from the use of a thing, then stockholders alone cannot be owners of corporate property. These arguments demonstrate that corporate property rights cannot be reduced to the individual property rights of stockholders.

One may think that the question of who owns the corporate property can be answered by simply adding the managers to the stockholders, and claiming that this new aggregate is the owner of the corporate property. Corporate property rights could then be reduced to the individual rights of the stockholders and the managers. I believe that this proposal has a germ of truth in it that is worth serious consideration. If control is the key ingredient in property rights then managers seem to have a legitimate claim to be owners of the corporate property, especially in large corporations where managerial prerogative is quite strong. In such stituations, managers have more control than all but a well-entrenched majority of stockholders.[27] But the nature of the property right which managers have is only distantly related to the property rights of individual human persons. These managers have not justly acquired a share in the corporation, indeed they are properly only high-level employees of that corporation.

Perhaps the strongest reason for thinking that managers do have some ownership claim in the corporation, and hence may constitute the missing element in the reduction of corporate property rights to the property rights of discrete individuals, is in the area of liability. Harms resulting from actions which can be properly ascribed to the corporation are increasingly said also to be the liability of individual managers of the corporation, although generally not the liability of the stockholders of the corporation.[28] But there are also liability limitations on managerial responsibility. If corporate property rights can be reduced to individual property claims, the individuals involved will be from disparate subgroups of the corporation and will have different types of claims.

To understand better the relationship between stockholders and managers in a given corporation, let me employ an analysis developed in chapter two. When a supervisor is authorized to give orders to an employee, that supervisor has been delegated to act for the corporation. The stockholders, or the board of directors, ultimately authorize these delegations. The authority of these individuals comes from the initial constituting acts through which the corporation first came into being. This causal nexus of actions must not be broken if the act of the employee is to be redescribed as the act of the corporation.

When someone is harmed by the actions of an employee of a corporation either the employee is liable individually or the corporation is liable. Normally, the employee is individually liable if he or she was acting outside the scope of authority bestowed on him or her by the higher-ranking members of the corporation standing for the whole corporation. If, instead, it can be shown that there has been a proper delegation of authority to the employee, then, in addition, the corporation itself would be subject to liability. What links the actions of the employee to the corporation is the causal nexus of acts from stockholders to managers to employees. The managers themselves can also be held liable on the same formula. If their actions were beyond their scope of authority then these actions were merely personal; if their actions were properly authorized then these actions implicate the corporation.

This neat way of ascertaining when a person's actions are the corporation's actions seemingly treats the corporation itself as a complex of individuals, bound together by various authorizing and delegating relations. But in the area of rights and duties incumbent on ownership, something is lost when we move from aggregate rights and duties of individual employees, managers, and stockholders to corporate rights and duties. Each individual is assigned a severely limited legal liability for what occurs within the proper confines of his or her role within the corporation. As I shall next show, the result of this limited liability for the individuals who constitute the corporation is that corporate liability itself is far more limited than is the liability of individual human owners of property.

It is a fact that American law provides limited liability for stockholders. Usually stockholder liability is limited to the amount the stockholder paid for his or her stock. As Richard Posner puts it: "The owner of a share of stock knows that whatever the debts the corporation may incur, he can at worst lose what he paid for his shares."[29] This limited liability is the chief incentive that individuals have for purchasing stock. But such a policy is not without its problems. Posner cites an example from New York state which illustrates one of the chief economic problems with limited liability.

> The owners of large fleets of cabs, in order to minimize accident liability, formed separate corporations for each cab. The only asset of each corporation was the cab it owned and the value of the cab was often less than the cost of the accident. The scheme largely eliminated the incentive to take cost-justified precautions and so fostered inefficiency.[30]

For most large corporations, no individual shareholder will have to provide personal funds to pay liability claims, thereby also eliminating the incentives that these individuals otherwise would have to take precautions. If there were no limited liability, the individual shareholders would have felt some incentive to be cautious, since failure to take precautions would result in bankruptcy. But the law, by providing limited shareholder liability, eliminates even the normal incentives to be cautious.

One attempt to set out a rigorous definition of common or corporate property recognized the importance of liability, as well as entitlement. Hoffman and Fisher suggest the following definition of common property:

> x is the common property of S1, S2, etc., if and only if S1, S2, etc., together have the right to exclude all others from the use or benefit

of x, and S1, S2, etc., each has the right not to be excluded from the use or benefit of x; BUT not the right to be excluded from liability for the maleficence of x.[31]

Hoffman and Fisher correctly indicate several important facts about all forms of collective property rights. First, as with all property rights there is what they call a "double-edged" character to claims which this right encompasses. There is both the claim of the owner to be able to exclude all others from the use or benefit of a thing, and also the claim of all nonowners to be excluded from liability from the maleficence of that thing. This point is vital in understanding the moral nature of property rights. What both owners and nonowners get from a system of property rights is a settled collection of rules about who may control and benefit from things, as well as about who has liability for the harms caused when those same things are controlled in such a way that harm results to nonowners. In a world without property rights, conflicts about benefits and liabilities are likely to arise which will not have easy solutions. This position is in line with the standard state of nature explanations of the justification of property rights in the liberal tradition, which hold that there must be sufficient benefits to individuals for any justification of a social practice, such as a property right.

Second, Hoffman and Fisher correctly point out that there must be not only joint exclusion of nonowners from benefit or control but also full inclusion of each member of the owning collective. If any member is excluded from benefit or use then that member is not properly a member of the group that collectively owns that thing. This is the point I stressed earlier when I said that corporate property rights were problematic because individual stockholders could be excluded from control of corporate assets. Hoffman and Fisher argue that "property is a right which necessarily takes the form of an individual right," just as I also argued that action is a characteristic form of behavior which also must be found in individual persons.

Property rights concern claims of individuals to exclude others and not to be excluded from certain benefits, as well as societal claims concerning which individuals have liabilities. I agree with Hoffman and Fisher that benefitting and being liable are moral concepts which are paradigmatically applied to individual persons. Just as corporate acting must ultimately make reference to the acting of individual persons due to the ontological status of action itself, so corporate property rights must ultimately make reference to the rights of individual persons due to the moral and legal status of the benefits and liabilities which have historically formed the core of the meaning of "property."

Hoffman and Fisher's definition of common property is not fully satisfactory, though, in two important respects, mainly due to ambiguities in that definition. They claim that "S1, S2, etc., together have the right to exclude all others." But what exactly do they mean by the term "together"? For the corporation, this cannot merely be an aggregate togetherness, for then the term "corporate property" would merely mean that each stockholder had full control over part of the assets of the corporation. Yet, this characterization will not capture the facts concerning the way the corporations are controlled. Instead, the way that members of a corporation (stockholders, managers, etc.) exercise exclusionary control is quite complex. To understand the way that stockholders and managers together control corporate assets requires that one understand such things as the organizational chart which outlines the flow of authority within that corporation from member to member. The members exercise control together insofar as they enable one another to do things they could not do on their own. But it is not true that all members together are involved, or have the right to be involved in every instance of control of corporate assets, and few of the members have similar roles in his process of control.

Second, Hoffman and Fisher are not as clear as they should be when they say that no member has the right to be excluded from liability. What is important is that the members, seen collectively, do not have the right to be relieved of liability for the negative consequences of the use of this property. It may be morally justifiable for each member to have his or her liability limited only to the share in the corporation (or the extent of involvement in the corporate decision) if it is also true that the sum total of the individual liabilities adds up to full responsibility spread throughout the group. But if the sum total of individual liabilities does not add up to full liability, as seems to happen when individual stockholder liability is set only at the value of investment, then the collectivity is relieved of full liability. And both of these collectively distributional possibilities are different from a noncollective distribution of liability which Hoffman and Fisher are trying to rule out. It remains unclear, for instance, who would have to pick up the difference after the liability had been distributed based on investment value alone. Must it be further divided among stockholders (or among managers?) for the liability condition to be met in their definition?

Hoffman and Fisher seem to think that corporate property, as a form of common property, should be readily reduced to individual property claims about benefits and social claims about individual liability. Yet they fail to understand that such a reduction must take into account a highly complex organizational structure in some corporations. For their analysis to be complete, Hoffman and Fisher need to specify more precisely the way in which the interrelationships of the members of a corporation affect that corporation's property rights.

I have been arguing that as in the case of corporate actions, corporate property rights should not be treated as isolatable from the exclusive claims of the individual members of the corporation to benefit from, or the claims of society that specifiable individuals be liable for, the effects of the property. Also, just as the corporation should not be said to act on its own behalf, so it should not be understood to have rights on its own behalf as some kind of superentity. Corporate property rights should be defined in terms of the complex and often varied ownership claims of the members who comprise the corporation. In terms of exclusivity of control, Hoffman and Fisher are correct in thinking that the members of the corporation must have the *prima facie* collective right to exclude nonmembers from decisions that affect the control of the corporate assets. But since each member is not given full control over any of these assets, the type of right which the member has should be viewed as significantly different in kind from traditional private property rights. Even more important is the status of liability in the corporation. As long as it is possible for the corporation to evade full liability because of the limited liability of its members, even taken collectively, then it is not possible to reduce corporate property rights to individual rights. As a result, corporate property rights should not be given the same moral or legal status as individual property rights. In chapter seven, section II, I shall draw out some of the policy implications of this argument.

Perhaps an analogy with private property would be helpful to illustrate this problem. If a guest falls through the rotting floor boards of my front porch, hitting his head as he falls, and thereby has a lengthy hospital stay to recuperate from his concussion, I would normally be liable for the medical bills he incurs. I am not relieved of this liability when the hospital bills exceed the original purchase price of my house or even its current market value. Rather, my liability extends to whatever is necessary to make him "whole." And even if this forces me into bankruptcy, my future wages may be attached. But in corporate property arrangements the case is quite different. If the same person falls on corporate premises and sustains the same injuries with the same hospital bills, the individual stockholders are liable only up to the value of their investment in the corporation. When the corporation has used up all of its assets in reimbursing the injured person for his hospital bills, it can merely declare bankruptcy and thereby end its liability. Legally there is no right to pursue reimbursement against the other assets of the stockholders.[32] The point is quite simple: by law stockholders have limited liability, whereas there is no corresponding limitation on liability that exists for the private homeowner.

Traditionally, there have been two ways of justifying the near total control over assets accorded to those individuals who own them. Either this unlimited control has been justified by reference to entitlement theory or desert theory. Because of the special status which corporate property rights currently occupy, neither of these justifications which apply to individual property rights can be easily extended to the corporate domain. Corporate property rights do not clearly protect the security or self-sufficiency of individuals, and they certainly don't guarantee that those who work hard will receive the benefits of their labor. The entitlement status of corporate property rights does not protect liberal democratic values of the stockholders or managers in any clear way. My earlier remarks on the curious status of the owners of corporations should make it clear why I think that these traditional values of individual property rights do not apply to corporate property.

Most importantly, stockholders (and managers as well) have limited liability in their corporations. Another way of putting this is that stockholders (and managers) collectively are not thought to deserve to bear full liability for harms that occur concerning their property. It seems reasonable to assume that these same people collectively are also not deserving of full rights of ownership, or what Proudhon called the right in a thing.[33]

What specific changes in legal policy are suggested by my arguments concerning the nonreducibility of corporate property rights to the property rights of individuals? The first change is that corporate property rights should not be treated as merely (and unambiguously) analogous to personal property rights. There really is no person hiding behind the fictitious corporate "person." Until the liabilities of stockholders and managers add up to the kind of full liability that real persons bear as property owners, then there should not be the same status given to corporate property as is given to individual property claims. I propose that we demote the status of corporate property in our society, making the list of possible restrictions on corporate property reflect the fact that this form of property does not have the moral support traditionally given to other property claims. Such a change in legal theory would take little effort. If the protection of some corporate property rights is shown to advance the protection of liberal values similar to the way that the protection of individual rights does, then those corporate rights should be given a correspondingly higher standing. If some other corporate property claims do not have this support, then they should be given a much lower status than is currently enjoyed. What would drop out altogether, though, is the presumption that normally accompanies other property claims in our society, namely, that these claims are *prima facie* overriding in situations where they are in conflict with other moral or legal claims. Corporate property rights cannot be justified in the same manner as the liberal tradition has justified other property rights; the law and morality should reflect this fact.

I conclude this chapter with a quotation from both a law professor and an economist, A. A. Berle and G. G. Means, who end their study of corporate property rights as follows:

> On the one hand, the owners of passive property, by surrendering control and responsibility over the active property, have surrendered the right that the corporation should be operated in their sole interest — they have released the community from the obligation to protect them to the full extent implied in the doctrine of strict property rights. At the same time, the controlling groups (the managers), by means of the extensions of corporate powers, have in their own interest broken the bars of tradition which require that the corporation be operated solely for the benefit of the owners of passive property. . . . They have placed the community in a position to demand that the modern corporation serve not alone the owners or the control (the managers) but all of society.[34]

6. Harming Groups

Throughout the first four chapters I argued that organized as well as unorganized groups can be said to act, to have intentions, and to be responsible for various harmful consequences. Now, in considering the harms and rights of social groups, it is again appropriate to ask whether the extent of organization is relevant for ascribing such moral concepts. In chapter five, I argued that both corporations and ethnic groups could be ascribed harm and rights. I suggested that corporate rights should not be given the same standing as individual rights; but I also suggested that harms to ethnic groups should sometimes be given priority over harms to individual humans. It is now time to examine in more detail the importance of organizational structure to the ascription of harm to groups.

I will first explain the harm that discriminatory policies produce in unorganized groups, and then I will explain the harm that results to corporations when their interests have been infringed. Along the way, I will argue that harm to unorganized groups should be given high standing because such harm necessarily entails harm to all members of the group. I will also argue that harm to organized groups such as corporations should not be given so high a standing as harm to unorganized groups since all of the members of a corporation are not necessarily harmed when these highly organized groups are harmed. The question of which policies for redressing these harms are most appropriate, as well as the question of adjudicating disputes between individual and group rights will be left to the final chapter.

I. Sexual Stereotypes and Group Harm

One difference between organized and unorganized groups is that harm directed at the group is more readily distributed to the individual members if the group is unorganized than if it is organized. The reason for this concerns the way that an unorganized group is normally harmed. Consider the case of the harm to the group Blacks from a policy of segregation in education which forces Blacks into inferior schools compared to those of whites. Since each Black child in the school district is unalterably Black, such a policy will harm and continue to harm all individuals of school age who are Black. On the other hand, consider the case of the harm to the Chrysler Corporation from a policy which restricted the free speech of Chrysler. Each member of the corporation will be harmed in the short-run to the extent that his or her well-being is connected to the economic well-being of the corporation. Yet, since the group is highly organized, harm will be distributed unevenly and some members of the group will be harmed very little. And, more importantly, since the identities of the members are not tied up with being members of Chrysler Corporation, the harm to individual members can be mitigated or eliminated when one ceases working at Chrysler. This difference will be shown to be significant in the following discussion.

One of the most common forms of harm to unorganized groups is negative stereotyping. Stereotyping of a group of persons occurs when a model or type is created from a composite of the characteristics of a few group members. All members of that group are indiscriminately perceived in terms of the model regardless of the extent to which each person fits the model or type. Negative stereotyping occurs when the model or type unjustifiably incorporates unfavorable characteristics. For a negative stereotype to become the basis for widespread patterns of harmful treatment, it is necessary that members of the group be easily distinguishable in ordinary social situations from persons who are not members of the group. It is then an empirical matter as to whether or not, in any culture, at any time, the existence of an easy distinguishability combined with a widely believed negative stereotype has, in fact, promoted unjustly harmful treatment. The existence of this sort of treatment constitutes a group-based harm. Any easily distinguishable group of persons could, under the right circumstances, be harmed in this way.

Webster's *New Twentieth Century Dictionary* (2nd ed., 1978) defines a stereotype as an "unvarying form or pattern, fixed or conventional expression, notion, character, mental pattern, etc., having no individuality, as though cast from a mold." Stereotypes are applied to members of human groups which are identified, for example, by race, sex, nationality, occupation, and sexual preference. These identifying features are regarded by people with stereotypic beliefs as if these group characteristics remained invariant throughout the group's population. A stereotype is thus a kind of generalization which treats the members of human groups as conforming to a pattern or mold. But unlike proper generalizations, a stereotype is resistant to counter-evidence. People who believe that Jews are cunning, for example, or that women are irrational, or that Blacks have a natural sense of rhythm will tend to overlook or discount those group members who do not fit the pattern. The nonconforming cases tend to be treated as exceptions to the rule, rather than as disconfirming evidence for the stereotype. In this way, the members of groups are treated as if they had no individuality, as if there were no salient differences among members of the same group.

Normally, stereotypes are bound up with evaluations, norms, and ideals. The traits associated with being a certain type of person are those which already have some negative or positive value. For example, a person will fear and avoid members of a group which has characteristics which are claimed to be threatening or loathsome. As a result, the norms and ideals embedded in stereotypes typically acquire a prescriptive force. Positive stereotypes function as ideals to which we expect the relevant group members to conform. For example, in American culture aggression is highly valued. Men are generally described as aggressive (and those men who aren't aggressive are told that they ought to be). Negative stereotypes curiously can also take on prescriptive force. People are sometimes denigrated for being better than they are expected to be, especially where "being better" is antithetical to the stereotype of the members of their group. Women are often condemned for excessive emotionality; yet individual women find themselves accused of hard-hearted frigidity when they are not as emotionally expressive as women in general are expected to be.

Stereotypes are not held as simple intellectual formulas; rather, they permeate attitudes, emotional reactions, and behavioral dispositions. The beliefs that one can articulate about the characteristics of a certain group are only the tip of a stereotype iceberg. First, there is also a heightened sensitivity to what one expects to find, and an insensitivity to what is strange and unexpected. Second, there is a readiness to react in what seem to be appropriate ways to the expected traits. For example, people will recount their change, refuse to give credit, or refuse to promote or hire another person because of a heightened readiness to react in certain ways to members of various groups. Third, some stereotypes elicit feelings as strong as fear and disgust concerning traits which members of certain groups are expected to display, even before they are displayed. As a result, it is very difficult to convince people on an intellectual level, on the level of statistics and data, that they have generalized incorrectly. Instead, overcoming stereotypes often involves a thorough retraining in the way one perceives and deals with one's world.

A stereotype may portray members of a group negatively in a variety of ways, for example, as incapable of performing occupations and tasks which are highly valued in the culture, as lacking esteemed dispositions or traits which are thought to characterize members of other groups, or as possessing dispositions or traits that are the objects of disapproval, ridicule, or contempt in the culture. Women have been thought, among many other unflattering things, to be unsuited for leadership positions, to lack various intellectual skills, and to be overly emotional and dependent. Confirming evidence of the existence of such stereotypes, found in the psychological and sociological literature, establishes a group-based vulnerability to harm of each and every member of the group "women."

It is important that stereotypes be recognized as social phenomena and not simply as the cognitive responses of individuals. Stereotypes become social phenomena when they are diffused throughout a culture. Henri Tajfel argues that social stereotypes are "derived from, and structured by, the relations between large-scale social groups of entities." In this capacity they contribute to "the creation and maintenance of group-ideologies explaining or justifying a variety of social actions" and they help "to preserve or create positively-valued differentiations of a group from other social groups."[1] The negative stereotype of women has been used, by contrast, to reinforce a positive evaluation of the group "men."

When a type of treatment is such that anyone who happens to be a member of a particular group (and who happens to meet the relevant conditions or be in the relevant circumstances at the right time) would have been treated that way regardless of her uniquely individual properties, then vulnerability to this type of treatment may be said to befall all the members of the group in question. In our culture, a wide range of harmful, restraining, and opportunity-denying treatments imposed particularly upon females, rather than males, are imposed in just this fashion.

For example, Philip A. Goldberg has conducted a number of studies which all point to the conclusion that women and men of college age have a lower expectation and assessment of the work of women than the work of men.[2] Goldberg concludes that "sexism approaches being a culturally fixed and almost universal attitude" and cannot be profitably investigated at "the level of individual psychology".[3] Helen Franzwa has done a content analysis of the stereotypes of women presented in contemporary women's magazines. She concludes that "the stories sampled in the women's magazines portray females as half persons who are completed and fulfilled only by a man."[4] Studies by Marie Groszko and Richard Morgenstern indicate that socializing institutions such as the family, media, and peer cultures are less likely to reinforce females than males for such personality traits as independence, initiative, curiosity, and originality,[5] and that institutions of higher learning continue to reinforce these "personality characteristics consistent with the feminine stereotype and fail to encourage those traits which allow one to become a competent and effective achiever."[6] The effects of such sterotypes can be seen in the studies which find that even academic psychologists rate male job applicants more highly than female applicants who have identical qualifications.[7]

Several different types of evidence confirm the occurrence of group-based harms to women due to negative stereotyping. First, there is evidence of direct harms to at least some members of the group. It is possible to identify specific individual group members who have suffered directly and to identify compensable harms which have been inflicted upon them. In the case of women, there is ample documentation of such direct harms. Evidence of sexual harassment in employment and education alone would suffice to make the case.[8]

Second, there is evidence of the sorts of interdependencies and interrelationships among the members of the group which would transmit to other group members further harms consequent upon the direct harms to some members of the group. Using ethnic groups as a model, there are three plausible interrelationships of this sort among women: shared group consciousness, confined primary relationships, and distinctive cultural heritage. This evidence indicates that the direct harms to some women lead to indirect harms to many other women,

with no evident limit to the total number who are affected by all
such cases.[9]

Most significantly, the assertion of group-based harms may also
be confirmed by evidence of a culturally pervasive negative stereotype
of the members of the group. In such a context, any group member
who dared to participate in a particular capacity, in a social realm
for which her group's stereotype is thought to make persons unsuited,
would suffer interference, ostracism, and, usually, outright exclusion
on the part of persons who are not members of her own group. It
hardly needs to be repeated that negative stereotypes with such far-
reaching significance have affected women in all aspects of public life
and most aspects of so-called private life as well. The empirical case
is overwhelming that women have suffered, and continue to suffer,
profound group-based harms in our culture.

The vulnerability to being treated according to an unjust stereotype is the vulnerability to being treated not as a unique individual
but only as a member of a group. The members of this group are
defined as having certain characteristics which many, if not most,
of the individuals may not have. To treat someone according to such
a stereotype is to disregard the individuality of the person so treated.
Thus, in an important sense the term "negative stereotype" loses its
sense when the group concept "women" is reduced to "individual
women a and b and c, etc." No analysis of the characteristics of these
individual women will reveal the characteristics of the stereotypical
image used by the given employer. And even if one could give these
characteristics in the description of that employer's attitudes toward
some given woman, one would still fail to capture the fact that such
attitudes will remain constant as the employer approaches woman after
woman, regardless of differences among them which should provide
empirical grounds for a change in his attitudes. The more general
point suggested by these considerations is the following:

(A) For each woman, a proper understanding of the harms of
sexual discrimination which she may have experienced requires reference to the group of women to which she belongs.
Though the harms befall her as an individual, they are
harms of a sort which are themselves "social" in the important sense that her group membership plays a role in her
victimization. In this sense, the harms of sexual discrimination can be said to befall women as a group.

An additive, or cumulative, account of the pervasiveness of sexual discrimination does not give adequate emphasis to the links between the various harms inflicted upon individual women, nor to the extent of that pervasiveness, nor to the pattern which emerges when those seemingly "individual" harms are grasped together. Consider the harms of discrimination against women in the paying workplace. The direct harms which some individual women have suffered have not befallen all women directly because in the past many women simply avoided participation in the public world of paid employment. For many such women, the avoidance of paid employment may be attributed to patterns of socialization which resulted in women themselves desiring to work exclusively in the domestic world of unpaid employment. Yet, for many other women, the choice to avoid the public workplace may also have been due to their recognition that their opportunities were severely curtailed by the reluctance, if not outright refusal, of employers to consider women as eligible or qualified job candidates. For all of these women who never directly experienced sexual discrimination on the job because they weren't on the job, it is still counterfactually true that *had* they attempted to compete in the paid workplace, they would have experienced direct sexual discrimination. All members of the group are indirectly harmed due to this risk. The net of indirect harms cast by the occasions of direct workplace sexual discrimination is far wider than the number of individual women who are affected directly by it.

Alan Goldman argues explicitly against the claim that all women are harmed when job opportunities are denied to some women by virtue of being women. Goldman contends that

> it might not be rational for everyone to desire a right to compete fairly for a job, as opposed to the availability of decent support without working. In that sense it can be maintained that those women who have chosen without pressure not to work have not been harmed even given the assumption that they would have been unjustly denied jobs had they applied.[10]

On the other hand, though, Goldman thinks that things are different for the denial of the opportunity to vote, since this is a good "which any rational person would rather have than not."[11]

Goldman's argument is unpersuasive. First, it is no argument against seeing some opportunity as a benefit to point out that one

has other opportunities one can get instead. Denial of a liberty option is the denial of a good regardless of whether one already has other
options or not. Second, Goldman assumes that housewives get support from their husbands without having to work, and thus have a
pretty good life already, not one which is disadvantaged. This position implies that housework is not "work" and also that having to
engage in housework to get support is a beneficial position to have
in a society. Yet, surely both of these points are false. Those who
engage in housework do work for a living, and generally work hard
for the support meted out to them. Merely because women have been
able to support themselves through housework tells us nothing that
would support Goldman's contention that public job opportunities
should not be seen as the kind of goods the deprivation of which constitutes a harm to these women. Furthermore, not being able to support themselves through public sector employment means that these
women are subjected to lower status "work" in their societies. Yet men
do not have to accept such lower-status jobs, since they do not encounter the barriers to high-status work based on their sex. Thus
women's traditional opportunities are not beneficial when compared
to the opportunities men have in our society.

When the various harms of sexual discrimination not related to
those of employment are added to those which are employment related,
the following point is suggested:

(B) It matters, for the proper understanding of the harms befall-
ing women as individuals, that so many individual women
have been harmed in similar ways, either directly or indirectly. Thus, even if the harms only befall individuals,
the social processes involved fail to be understood properly
unless the many individual-befalling harms are seen to instantiate a pervasive pattern.

The pattern which emerges harkens back to the previous point about
stereotyping. The deprivation of opportunities to compete equally in
the workplace, whether or not actually recognized by each woman
through efforts to compete in that realm and whether or not grasped
consciously by each woman, was (and, in too many cases, continues
to be) predicated upon membership in the group "women." This
deprivation of opportunity, through negative stereotyping and restrictive employment practices, is thus properly characterized as a group-
based harm to women.

Such a group-based harm should be afforded high-standing in any hierarchy of harms in a given community since the number of people potentially affected is quite large, and since it is not possible for the people potentially affected to avoid easily, if at all, these effects. Unlike individual harms, group-based harms are guaranteed to have wide scope, especially when the group in question is unorganized. In such cases, the group is treated by picking out characteristics of group membership as a means of identifying who will be harmed. But when a group is unorganized, the group is identified by the same characteristics used to identify its individual members. For organized groups, this is not necessarily the case, since the decision-making structure or other aspects of the organization could be the basis for identifying the group for harmful treatment.

I have been arguing that harm does distribute readily to the members of an unorganized group when such a group is harmed. Unorganized groups are identified by reference to common characteristics of the individual group members. There is often a type of structure to unorganized groups which allows them to act, but the adverse treatment of an unorganized group is normally accomplished by restrictions affecting what is common to all members. In the case of biologically identified unorganized groups, such adverse treatment will necessarily affect the individual members because what is common to the group is also unalterably a characteristic of each member.

I will argue next that corporations and other organized groups should not have the same protections against harm as individual humans (or unorganized groups) since harm to organized groups does not necessarily mean that individual humans will be unalterably harmed. In the case of free speech, it is not necessarily true that restrictions on the speech of corporations means that the individual human members of the corporation are restricted in their speech. Harm does not necessarily distribute to the individual members of a group when an organized group is harmed, since the identities of the individual members of organized groups are not tied up with group membership.

This points to two distinct ways that groups can be harmed. They can be harmed either by adversely affecting their structures, and thereby adversely affecting their ability to act; or they can be harmed by adversely treating their members according to a characteristic which is also a group-defining characteristic. Organized groups are normally harmed in the first way, but unorganized groups, since their structure is difficult to identify, are normally harmed in the second way. This is why I have claimed that harm to unorganized groups normally distributes to the individual members, whereas this is not necessarily the case in harm to organized groups.

Thus, in cases where the rights of groups conflict with the rights of individuals, it matters whether the group is organized or unorganized. When the group is unorganized, then the group-harm is quite likely to distribute into harm to all of the members. In this case, the group-harm is more important than is the individual harm, and the conflict should be resolved in favor of the group. When the group is organized, then the individual members of the group will not necessarily be harmed and the conflict need not be resolved in favor of the group.

Chapter seven resumes this discussion by considering some political and legal remedies that have been proposed to redress group-harm. In that chapter I will complete the above argument by showing that a concern for rights may sometimes call for supporting strategies which are group-oriented rather than individual-oriented, thereby siding with the unorganized group over an individual in conflict situations. But first I will examine more closely the harm that befalls organized groups, such as business corporations, when their speech is restricted.

II. Corporate Harms and Free Speech Rights

It has been recently argued that corporations can be harmed in such similar ways to that of individual human persons that these corporations should be afforded, under the United States Constitution, the same rights protection that human persons have. While it does make sense to say that corporations can be harmed, this harm is not equivalent to that which befalls humans, and hence corporations are not deserving of the same rights protection under the Constitution that humans have.

A recent Supreme Court decision which argued for the similarity between human and corporate harm was *First National Bank* v. *Bellotti*. Massachusetts passed a statute which prohibited any political expression by corporations on matters not directly related to the business or assets of the corporation. Several corporations brought suit against the state of Massachusetts challenging the constitutionality of this restriction of corporate speech. These corporations wished to express opinions on a proposed state referendum concerning a graduated personal income tax. The statute restricting corporate speech was not overturned until it reached the United States Supreme Court where a bare majority of the justices held that the State of Massachusetts had indeed violated the corporations' freedom of expression. Justice Powell, writing for the majority, argued that the value of free speech does not depend on the source of that speech, whether it be a corporation or an individual human being.[12]

Corporations should be granted rights to free speech, but it is my view that certain legal restrictions on these rights, beyond those which affect individual free expression, are morally permissible, constitutionally legitimate, and, perhaps, even morally justified. Two of the primary rationales for individual free speech are that it enhances autonomy and promotes true and informed beliefs on the part of human beings. I will consider whether the legal protection of corporate speech could accomplish anything comparable to this in regard to corporations. If not, then a powerful argument for protecting corporate expression will be eliminated. Finally, I will argue that the legal protection of corporate expression frequently conflicts with individual expression. This consideration casts great doubt on the advisability of extending the same free speech protections to corporations that have been traditionally extended to human beings.

Certain preliminary remarks are in order. The discussion will be mainly focused on large, for-profit corporations. Also, it will be assumed, as is common in constitutional theory, that individual speech is the paradigm of constitutionally protected speech. This means that the justification for protecting human expression provides us with a paradigm for understanding the protection of nonhuman expression. But it also means that if the protection of corporate speech were to interfere with human speech, then there would be a *prima facie* case *against* protecting the corporate speech. The burden of proof would, in that case, shift to those who wish to protect the two sorts of expression equally.

Human individuals benefit in various ways from the legal protection of their expression. They have greater opportunities for learning the truth about matters which concern them; they grow in autonomy through the opportunities to express their own views and grasp for themselves the impact of these expressions on others; they acquire dignity for being articulately contributing members of the communities in which they live. As a result, human individuals would be harmed if they were deprived of free speech. The legal right to the protection of expression derives its justification, at least in part, from the benefits to individuals which are the consequences of this protection.[13]

There is another way that free speech can be supported other than by the consequentialist argument above. Rather than looking to the effects of not protecting free speech, one could claim that it is essential to being a person that the principle of free speech remain in place.[14] Such a deontological justification of free speech protection could be applied to corporations only if corporations have the features which humans have, in virtue of which having free speech is essential. Here the chief feature would be autonomy. Because of this, the following discussion of corporate autonomy is relevant to deontological as well as consequentialist discussions of the harms resulting from the denial of free speech rights.

In the previous chapter I argued that the corporation has a moral status different from that of individual human beings, so, too, the harms it suffers are narrower and more restricted than are harms to human individuals. Could corporations be harmed in terms of the *specific* interests which are encompassed by the free speech protection of the First Amendment? That is, are there corporate analogues of the individual interests in autonomy and in true and informed belief?

Autonomy is a matter of self-rule, a matter of living by values and principles of one's own. An autonomous person does not think or act at the direction or control of others; rather, she works out for herself what is to be done based on standards which are, in some sense, her own. The greater a person's autonomy, the more she encompasses within herself the principles and motivations which immediately underlie her choices and her actions, and the less she is under the control of other agents. This is why autonomy is highly prized as a personal attribute in our individualistic culture.[15]

Most importantly, in hearing a diversity of opinions, and in being able to test one's assessment of them in a process of free and open interchange with others, one develops critical skills, a sense of certitude, and convictions of one's own. Autonomy is greatly facilitated by, and is at least partly realized in an array of capacities which encompass articulate reflection. When one considers an individual human being, one can easily imagine the range of activities which will promote her autonomy and the sort of independence of mind in which she will manifest and realize her autonomy. There is a rich and diverse notion of what it is for an individual to rule herself and to be free of the domination and control of other agents. The case is more complex and less obvious when we turn to corporations. The most immediate problem is that it is difficult to conceptualize the nature of the corporate "self" which might autonomously *rule* itself, and which might facilitate this rule through speech.

The corporation is an organized group of persons who are interrelated formally and hierarchically and who carry out joint ventures. Certain of the actions of these persons integrate in various ways to constitute the ongoing behavior of the corporation. Individual human actions are the (vicarious) actions of the corporation. To restate one of the theses of chapter five, it is the sort of self whose actions must be embodied in the action of its members, each of whom is already a whole coherent person and whose actions already cohere as the actions of a person.

What does autonomy mean for a "self" such as this? Human groups of all sorts may clearly aspire to autonomy *as groups*. Nation-states, the several states and provinces within a state, trade unions, religious sects, fraternal and sororal associations, sewing circles, quilting bees — and corporations — all endeavor to be free of external coercion and control, and to carry on their activities in the light of their own values. Organized group activities will more readily evolve into a group's *own* activities if the group, in some sense, is free to evaluate prevailing standards of how its activities ought to be carried out, and to develop its own principles. A system of free and open expression will facilitate this process. To be sure, the critical reflection and the development of new principles will be carried out *vicariously* by any group, through, and by means of, the critical and creative reflections of its individual members. Nevertheless, it makes sense to understand human groups of all kinds, including corporations, as having the potential for a *kind* of autonomy expressing itself through the ways in which they carry out their joint ventures, and hence as having a collective autonomy.

However, does the corporate interest in autonomy justify the legal protection of corporate speech in the same way that the protection of individual human speech is justified? For a number of reasons

I believe that the answer is no. First, legal traditions are already in place for the governmental regulation of certain forms of corporate expression, which, if they were the expressions of individuals would be considered harmful. Corporations, unlike individuals, are not afforded the privilege against self-incrimination;[16] and corporations, unlike individuals, are restricted in the contributions they can make in federal elections. Few if any critics of governmental regulation challenge these restrictions. Justice Rehnquist argues persuasively that these restrictions do not adversely affect corporate well-being.[17] Thus, restrictions on corporate expression are already widely accepted that do not raise challenges on grounds of corporate autonomy.

Second, corporate autonomy is not intrinsically valuable in the way in which individual autonomy is intrinsically valuable. Corporate autonomy is *instrumentally* valuable to the corporation's members in their collective pursuit of the corporation's goals. This contrasts with the view of autonomy as an intrinsically valuable ingredient of the fulfilled individual human life, a view often taken by deontological theorists. The restricted goals of for-profit corporations center around economic profit-making; it is not essential that the profits be made autonomously. A corporation has still fulfilled its *raison d'etre* even if its profits are made at the direction and control of other agents, such as hired accountants and lawyers or the human inventors whose designs are incorporated into a company's products.

Third, individual members of corporations remain individual persons who can express themselves outside of the corporate domain. Restrictions on corporate speech do not directly harm individual humans by preventing them from expressing themselves as individuals. Individual autonomy is not necessarily infringed by a lack of constitutional protection for corporate expression. There are situations, to be sure, in which individuals have a common interest in expressing themselves collectively, by means of a group's vicarious expression. This is especially true of people who have little financial resources or social status, and have limited access to means of expression. By combining together in great numbers, they can sometimes make their political grievances heard and their needs known. Certain landmark free speech cases of the 1950s, involving the NAACP, were of this sort.[18] A collectivity which organizes specifically to advance the social and political well-being of a group of persons who are individually incapable of doing so must *essentially* participate in wide-ranging forms of political speech—the paradigm of constitutionally protected expression—in order to achieve its aims. This is not the case with a for-profit corporation.

Profit-seeking goals are, of course, advanced by *commercially* related speech, that is, by advertising, and by political speech which is relevant to the business activities of the corporation. But these are exactly the forms of expression left *un*restricted by the Massachusetts statute. In the *Bellotti* case, the First National Bank of Boston and other financial corporations tried to influence voters to disapprove a referendum which would have authorized the legislature of Massachusetts to enact a graduated income tax. Corporate autonomy, in the realm of expression *pertaining to corporate endeavors*, would have been left untouched even if this speech were to have been prohibited.

The legal system of free expression has also be defended on the alternative ground that human beings benefit from it not simply as speakers but also as *hearers* of the protected speech. A system of free speech gives people greater opportunity to hear diverse points of view, and, hence, greater opportunity to hear the truth and to choose more wisely as a result.[19] Alexander Meiklejohn has extended this argument by pointing out that the exercise of free speech is necessary for the promotion of self-government.[20] This argument, it should be noted, is advanced not as a defense of *corporate* rights to free speech; rather it is an appeal to the rights of *individuals* to hear a diversity of views, and by becoming informed these individuals can make judgments and participate in a democratic political process. As with the autonomy argument, if Meiklejohn's argument could be applied to corporate speech, there would be a *prima facie* case in favor of allowing all forms of corporate expression.

There are several reasons for thinking that the above argument does not work. First, restricting corporate speech, in such domains as that of political expression, does not prevent corporation members from expressing their views *as individuals*. Under such restrictions, people would generally not be deprived of any of the ideas these individuals would otherwise express. Hence, the public's right to hear diverse views would not be infringed by restrictions on corporate political speech. What would happen is that corporate members would be prevented from using corporate funds and the corporate name and image to *support* their own individual expression.

The reason for saying that the dissemination of political ideas is not likely to be adversely affected by restrictions on corporate speech stems in large part from an empirical fact. Those who are most influential in corporate decision-making are also those who are in the wealthier class of people in America. Unlike such groups as the NAACP, large, for-profit corporations are not influenced by those individuals who have trouble getting their voices heard in the political arena. When a corporation is restricted from engaging in speech, the leaders of that corporation generally have the personal resources to make their ideas known to the public. There will be an adverse impact on the dissemination of political ideas, *in some cases*, because, for instance, saturation campaign advertising, largely a function of huge capital investment well beyond the means of any but the largest corporations, will be less likely when such corporate speech restrictions are in place. On the other hand, if the members of the NAACP were to be restricted from pooling resources, under their organization's name, in order to engage in political speech, it is unlikely that those political ideas would receive significant dissemination. My position is that when laws deny legal protection to certain sorts of corporate political speech, there is nothing lost *which deserves protection under the First Amendment*.

Second, it is *individual* speech which would be expressed under the corporate banner in those cases in which the topic was a matter unrelated to corporate business or assets. Any views which do not pertain to the economic enterprises of a for-profit corporation are *by definition* not covered by the corporate charter or other corporate statements of purpose. They truly would be nothing more than the views of individuals who happen to be corporation members. The public's right to hear diverse views does *not* extend so far as to include legal protection for those individuals who would use corporate resources to express their own ideas. Edwin Rome and William Roberts echo these views in *Corporate and Commercial Free Speech:*

> The question of the power of a corporation to make expenditures for political purposes would appear to turn on the subsidiary question of whether the particular expenditure is reasonably connected to the best interests of the corporation.

> [In *Cort* v. *Ash*, 422 US 66 1975,] the Supreme Court suggested that state law remedies might exist for waste of corporate assets or for breach of fiduciary duty, or for *ultra vires* conduct by corporate directors.[21]

Third, while hearing a diversity of opinions is important for self-government, and this will normally justify granting corporations free speech rights, there is a counterveiling detriment to self-government which arises from unrestricted corporate political speech. At least since the turn of the century it has been recognized that large organizations have the potential to drown out the speech of most individual persons in the political process. The *prima facie* justification of corporate political speech is most clearly offset by the risk that it will overwhelm individual speech in those cases where the corporate actors have no material interest in the political question at issue, since this corporate speech is not likely to add much new to the debate.

There are at least two salient facts about the ontology and agency of corporations which make their entitlement to freedom of expression a peculiar one. Corporations are hierarchically related to the individuals whose speech is the paradigm of that which deserves legal protection. This means that corporations do not exist as agents who are separate from the individuals who are already protected speakers in the marketplace of ideas. Rather, human individuals have created and sustained those corporate "entities" through various legal procedures governing the interactions of certain human individuals. And as Justice White concluded in his dissenting opinion in the *Bellotti* case, "the state need not permit its own creation [the corporation] to destroy it."

Corporations represent a type of what some theorists call "voluntary associations" among human individuals. By creating these associations, human beings become socially organized into functional groups which themselves operate and interact within the larger social order. If these associations are expressive moral agents in their own right, then they will have points of view and things to say which may conflict in various ways with the points of view of human individuals and the things that human individuals want to say. Furthermore, the very nature of the protections which associational, or corporate, speech requires may systematically conflict with the nature of the protections required for the expressive freedom of human individuals.

Thomas Emerson, in *The System of Freedom of Expression*,[22] has focused on two possible sorts of conflict which may arise for a system of speech protection which covers voluntary associations as well as human individuals. First, there may be conflicts between the rights of association members and the rights of the association's officials.

These conflicts may arise either when these officials act in their capacity as agents or representatives of the association or when they act as individuals (with associational power to enforce their individual viewpoints). Second, there may be conflicts between the association which seeks to express itself and (some of) its members who disapprove of this speech. This is especially problematic when the resources of the members are used to finance or support those associational expressions.

The conflict between the expressive interests of human individuals and the interests of the voluntary associations which many of them comprise is not analogous to the conflicts which might arise between the expressive interest of different human individuals. Organized associations of human individuals only have opinions and express themselves vicariously; whereas discrete human individuals do not have to employ this intermediate mode of expression. Humans are paradigmatic expressive agents because of their ontologically basic status as expressive agents. Conflicts among individual human speakers are conflicts among entities at the same ontological level.

Associations and organizations, by contrast, are composed of individuals, each of whom is already an expressive agent. Organizations rarely have points of view which unanimously represent the views of their members. Corporations acquire points of view through the interpretation and application of the charter by leading members or agents of the corporation, such as members of the board of directors or top-level executives and managers. Unanimous concurrence of all members is almost never required to endorse these corporate points of view before efforts are made to express them.

Thus, conflicts may arise because some corporate members express views which their corporations attempt to suppress, or because corporations express views which members wish not to support. The free expression of human individuals is being *prima facie* violated when their expressive efforts are suppressed even by those very associations to which they "voluntarily" belong, or when other associations to which they make financial or other contributions express points of view which they do not wish to support. The harm done to corporations when their speech is curtailed is not more important than the harm done to individual humans when this same corporate speech is left uncurtailed.

A different sort of free speech conflict which might arise between human individuals and corporations centers on the effects of large concentrations of wealth and power on the democratic process.[23] Corporations have the potential for becoming very powerful "members" of society at large. As Justice White argued, in his dissent in the *Bellotti* case, wealthy corporations "control vast amounts of economic power, which may, if not regulated, dominate not only the economy but also the very heart of our democracy, the electoral process."[24] These possibilities for controlling vast economic resources and commensurately vast political power, depend at least in part, on the legal protections afforded to corporations in our society.

Corporations are legal creations — but they are creations which can sometimes acquire the power to dominate the social realms in which they participate and to overwhelm the power of all other agents. Because these associations are state-legitimized creations of the individuals in a given society, it seems not unreasonable for the state to restrict the power of such entities so that they do not use their state-legitimized wealth and power to dominate unfairly the arena of political discussion and decision-making. Various government statutes have had this aim. The Corrupt Practices Act, originally enacted in 1907, has, for example, restricted corporate contributions in federal elections.[25]

It is also true that extremely wealthy and powerful individual humans can dominate the electoral process. Of course, these individuals are not normally in such economically powerful positions because of explicit state action protecting their interests in a privileged way compared to that of other humans, as is true for corporations. Also, to restrict the speech of wealthy individuals would have an adverse impact on the speech of those other individuals who are not wealthy. We find ourselves in an area where interests must be balanced, and should recognize that doing so is a well-accepted constitutional strategy. While some individual human speech may harm the democratic process as much as corporate political speech, other interests tip the balance in favor of allowing potentially harmful speech by wealthy individual humans. But since there are not the same interests on the side of corporate political speech, the balance is tipped in favor of protecting the political process from possible domination by large corporations.

Political speech pertains, among other things, to the electoral process; corporations are not sovereign participants in that process. Individuals must decide for themselves how to vote and how to participate in our democratic form of government because ultimately individual human beings are the source of political authority. Political speech is the forum in which people work out, each for herself, what political choices they will make. If it weren't for our ultimate political sovereignty, then our political speech would lack the constitutional importance it now has. And precisely here we find another major contrast between individuals and corporations: corporations are not, as such, sovereign members of our civil society. They exist at the sufferance of law and judicial ruling, and not as being the *ultimate sovereign authorities of* our legislative and judicial systems. On the other hand, individual human beings, who are such agents, remain free to express their political opinions *as individuals*, even in a system which restricts corporate political expression. Hence, individual free speech would not, in such a system, be infringed by the restrictions on corporations.

Let us look to the example of restrictions on a corporation's *commercial* speech to get an idea of what may be legitimately restricted concerning a corporation's *political* speech. In American law, there are already legal restrictions on commercial speech, for example, truth in lending laws and regulations against false advertising. If *commercial* speech, which is necessary to corporate survival, can be the legitimate subject of legal restrictions, then *political* speech, especially on matters not germaine to corporate business, can also legitimately be restricted.

Thus, there are several reasons for positively restricting the kind of corporate political speech which was the subject of the *Bellotti* case. First, corporations are constituted out of human individuals whose speech is already protected. This ontologically dependent relationship creates the empirical possibility for conflict between the unrestricted speech of corporations and the free speech rights of their individual human members. Second, the potential for vast corporate wealth creates the empirical possibility that corporations can overwhelm individuals in the arena of expression. Third, corporations are not entities with either a moral or constitutional *prima facie* entitlement to the legal protection of their expression;[26] corporations are not politically sovereign. Given the empirical potential for corporate expression to interfere with individual human expression, and given that individual human expression, unlike that of corporations, *prima facie* deserves legal protection, it is, therefore, justifiable to place restrictions on the political speech of corporations, even to the point of restrictions which would be intolerable or unjustifiable if applied to individual human beings. For these reasons, the Supreme Court's decision in *First National Bank of Boston* v. *Bellotti* should be rejected. Corporate harm, at least that harm which arises from curtailment of corporate political speech, is simply less important than harm to individual human persons.

7. Justice for Groups

In chapter six, I argued that the rights of corporations should be given a lower status than they are normally afforded, especially when the rights of the corporation to speak conflict with the rights of individuals to express themselves and to exercise political power. I also argued that the rights of unorganized groups such as women or Blacks, should be given a higher status than they are normally afforded. This is especially plausible when the rights of women or Blacks in such areas as employment, from which they have been historically restricted, conflict with the rights of individuals who have not been the subject of past harmful treatment.

Such arguments call for an investigation of what justice requires when there are conflicts between the putative rights or interests of groups and the rights or interests of discrete individuals. In this final chapter, I will attempt to provide the beginning of an answer to this important question. Since so much has been written on the nature of justice in the last twenty years, I cannot hope to survey all of the leading views of justice. I will confine most of my discussion to the narrow question of whether respect for the rights of discrete individual humans requires that group-oriented political and legal strategies be abandoned. I argue that it does not. In so arguing, I provide support for those group-oriented political and legal strategies which have been proposed to redress harms to groups.

In the first section, I take up the arguments of the legal theorist Marshall Breger who has argued that when resources are diverted from the needs of individuals to the needs of a group, injustice often results. He claims that when federal funds are used for group impact litigation strategies, such as in the class action suit, there is a violation of the rights of individual poor persons whose legal problems are different from those of the class. But it will be shown that a concern for rights can be quite consistent with such strategies as the class action suit, even when resources are scarce. I dispute the contention that, in cases of conflict, only a random selection method meets the requirements of justice in deciding which legal cases to accept.

In the second section, I argue that organizations, such as the NAACP, which seek to secure the rights of groups of otherwise disenfranchised individuals, should be given special political and legal standing. I then attempt to reconcile this claim with that of the previous chapter concerning the rights to free speech of business corporations. When an organized social group advances the rights or interests of disadvantaged individuals, then it should be supported by political and legal strategies even if those strategies adversely affect certain individuals. But if an organized social group does not advance this objective, it is much more reasonable to support the rights and interests of individuals over those of the organized group. Only in exceptional cases does justice dictate that the rights of organized groups be favored over the rights of individuals.

I. Class Action Suits and Rights Conflicts

Marshall Breger has voiced perhaps the most detailed philosophical objections to group impact decision procedures employed in poverty law programs. Although many of his arguments have been made by earlier theorists, he brings together the chief conceptual points that such individualists have used to criticize publicly funded group litigation for the poor. Breger's arguments[1] can be summarized as follows:

(1) The judicial process in America is a monopoly, due to control by the state. This limits the extent to which individuals can successfully resolve disputes on their own.

(2) The right to counsel is a procedural right which guarantees that individuals have access to the legal process. Without counsel, individuals would be at a great disadvantage in the monopolistic legal system.

(3) The right to access to the legal system, which entails the right to counsel, is an entitlement based on what is due each and every citizen of a country that has a monopoly on the legal system; these rights are not merely socially useful devices.

(4) Rights can only be overridden by other rights claims. All

denials of a right must have another (or the same) strong competing right as the basis for their justification. A mere increase in social utility is never strong enough to override an individual's right to legal access.

(5) Since there are not, and are unlikely ever to be, sufficient funds to provide legal counsel to all who cannot afford it, someone's legal access rights will always be denied. But, considerations of group impact or utility cannot be used to determine which persons are to receive the benefits these funds afford. Any such numerical calculation violates the basic entitlements and dignity of those individual poor persons thereby deprived of legal access.

(6) In scarcity situations, failure to provide for each person's access right is not necessarily a denial of respect for these citizens as persons. A system of distribution that puts equal weight on each potential client's complaint maintains respect for persons. Group impact allocation systems, insofar as they put unequal weight on some individual complaints, fail to respect the rights of poor persons.

I agree with Breger that the state has an effective monopoly over the court system in America. This means that most attempts to resolve problems through private means are stymied by the fact that one party can always appeal to a court of law and force the other party to renegotiate through the state-run process. I also agree that if one does not have legal counsel in this state-run system of justice, one is at a great disadvantage. The legal process in America is inordinately complex and the methods of pleading are generally not comprehensible even to well-educated citizens. Yet, while each citizen does have a right of access to the court system, and this does entail a right to counsel even in civil cases, Breger is mistaken in assuming that this right is merely procedural in nature.

The flaw in Breger's argument lies in his contention that any group-oriented calculations violate the access rights of those poor people thereby denied legal services. Breger claims to derive this position from the assumption that only rights claims can override other rights claims. I agree that rights generally should not be overridden by mere considerations of utility. But I fail to see why rights theory would rule out scarce resource allocation procedures that attempt to maximize the fulfillment of access rights claims. I will support the contrary contention that at least some group impact case selection procedures do not fall prey to the standard rights-based arguments against utility calculations employed by Breger. To reach this conclusion, I will first dispute the contention advanced by Breger that rights theory requires that exactly equal treatment would not maintain respect for persons. Furthermore, I argue that group-impact allocation procedures need not be seen as utilitarian if their purpose is to maximize rights fulfillment rather than preference satisfaction. Proponents of equal access to the legal system should come to agree that some group-impact case selection procedures are compatible with a concern for the rights of poor persons.

Procedural Rights and Welfare Rights

When the OEO first funded a legal services program in 1970, the mandate given to this program was to "ensure use of the judicial system and the administrative process to effect changes in laws and institutions which unfairly and adversely affect the poor."[2] Thus, from the beginning, the federally funded poverty law program in America was directed to serve the interests of the poor as a group, not simply individual clients who merely happened to be poor. The chief practical reason for this is that Congress has never been willing to fund fully all of the legal needs of poor persons. Goodman and Walters pointed out that

> [in] 1975 there were approximately 11.2 lawyers for every 10,000 persons above the federal poverty line. Even with over $100 million in federal subsidies, there was less than one lawyer for every 10,000 people below the poverty line. Only about 15% of the legal problems of the poorest segment of the population receive any kind of legal attention.[3]

The scarcity of legal counsel makes it plausible that some type of collective resource allocation procedure is warranted so that the number of legal problems of the poor that are able to be handled by available services is increased.

One of Breger's assumptions is that access rights, and the right to counsel entailed by them, are of a higher standing than welfare concerns such as eliminating poverty. According to him, it is an unjustified denial of access rights to turn clients away based merely on such welfare considerations. Yet Breger offers no convincing argument to show that we should conceive of things in this way. Why is not welfare also something which is a matter of right in American society? Why should the right to subsistence food and housing be seen as less important than the right to equal access to the legal process? And why cannot the right to equal access itself be justified by reference to welfare considerations?

According to Breger, rights are individualistic in that they are justified independently of, and are often opposed to, the collective goals of the community. He claims that to "say that X has a right to Y is to give X a claim to Y regardless of the utility of doing so."[4] Yet, this does not immediately rule out the possibility that both equal access and welfare are rights. Breger admits this point, but he maintains that if this is so, it is nonetheless true that equal access and welfare are rights of very different types. In Breger's view

> The right to legal assistance has been declared an "inherent right of a citizen" in that "individuals" can hardly be expected to live under and respect the law unless they have an opportunity to use it." Thus the right to counsel may be defined as a civil or juridical right rather than a welfare right.[5]

Such civil rights are granted to citizens to protect their political interests,[6] whereas a welfare right is a social right of the sort that rights to adequate food, shelter, and clothing are. Breger is justifiably wary of recognizing welfare rights, but nothing in his position rules out this possibility.

Yet, if Breger admits that there are welfare rights, such as the right to have sufficient food, shelter, and clothing, he must then explain why appeals to such rights cannot justify denials of equal access rights. His position seems to be that "inherent rights of citizens" are more important than mere "welfare rights," because if individual citizens do not have their civic freedoms guaranteed above all else, democratic decision making cannot take place. But, it seems implausible that an individual's right to obtain counsel is generally more important than one's right to sufficient food, shelter, and clothing (welfare rights). To paraphrase an argument by Henry Shue, if basic economic needs are not met, there is nothing to prevent a government from holding one's other rights hostage in exchange for those economic necessities.[7] Some economic rights are as basic to our security from governmental tyranny as are certain political or civil rights. Indeed, the main conceptual distinction should be between those political or economic rights which are basic to security and those political or economic rights that are not.[8] Without the protection of all our basic rights, the protection of procedural rights alone will have little effect.

Moreover, those access rights which are vitally important for the maintenance of our system of government are both politically and economically basic. They are politically basic insofar as they provide the means of each citizen to express himself or herself through the chief political mechanism of conflict resolution. But they are also economically basic in that they provide, especially for the poor, the legal means to defend their basic economic interests (more importantly those concerning food, housing, and income) against those who hold economic power in the society.

The conceptual distinction between procedural rights and welfare considerations begins to break down when it is recognized that some procedural rights are important for economic as well as political reasons. It is then possible to argue that basic procedural rights, such as the poor's right to equal access to the legal system, are themselves at least partially justified by reference to collective economic well-being, that is by reference to welfare considerations. Furthermore, basic economic rights, such as the right to subsistence food, clothing, and shelter, are also at least partially justified by reference to political or procedural justice for the individuals who happen to be poor. Thus, claims to equal access rights cannot be supported independently of welfare considerations, and certainly they are not opposed to welfare considerations. It may then be argued that not all calculations which look to the collective goals of a community of poor persons are unalterably opposed to the access rights of individual poor persons. It is not implausible to believe that equal access rights can be the subject of allocation schemes that are oriented toward the collective goals of a group of poor persons. However, some may suggest that concern for individual dignity requires that random allocation schemes which center on individual cases be used, even if a concern for equal access does not.

Equal Opportunity and Case Selection Procedures

A number of authors writing about scarce medical resources have argued in a similar vein with Breger that respect for the individual transcendent dignity of each person requires that these persons be provided equal opportunity to receive scarce resources. James Childress, for instance, has argued that a "first come, first served" or lottery method of allocating scarce lifesaving medical resources is the only way to preserve respect for persons and human dignity.[9] He claims that if we take into account who each person is, what contributions that person is likely to make to the social good, or what responsibilities that person has to family, or friends, or even the nation in deciding to whom to give lifesaving medical resources, we fail to give each person that respect which each deserves merely by being human. The utilitarian considerations submerge what is transcendent and unique about each person into that person's social role, thereby denying to each person the dignity that should be afforded to him or her alone. Equal opportunity and equal rights, so it is claimed, cannot be preserved through such utilitarian distributional schemes.

I will advance two arguments against the equal opportunity critique of utilitarian calculations used in the allocation of scarce resources. First, equal opportunity does not entail radical equality of treatment, that is, exactly equal treatment of each person. Second, the cases of medicine and law are not formally analogous in any event, precisely because of the ability of a lawyer to handle more than one client's problems through one suit. While Breger does not support totally random decision procedures in legal services allocation, consideration of Childress' stronger position will allow us to see what is at stake more clearly when equal opportunity arguments are advanced against utilitarian calculation schemes.

If two people apply for a job it is not more protective of their individual dignities to flip a coin to decide whom to hire than to determine which person best meets a rational set of criteria designed to pick the best worker. Concern for equality and respect for persons, as Ronald Dworkin and others have argued at great length, does not necessarily entail exactly equal treatment.[10] Indeed, exactly equal treatment (in this case, an exactly equal chance of getting the scarce job) fails to take account of just those personal differences which must be considered if people are to be treated as unique and autonomous members of a moral community. Treating people as if there were no differences between them does not respect their individuality. Random methods take no account of personal circumstance, degree of need or merit, as well as a host of other factors based on uniqueness of individuals. It is true that irrelevant differences among persons should not be used as a basis for distinguishing among them. But not all differences are irrelevant to modes of treatment such as hiring practices. Random selection procedures completely fail to capture any of the relevant differences among persons and hence treat these persons as mere faceless numbers, hardly a practice which generally would preserve or protect individual dignity.

Childress argues that any attempt to provide nonmedical criteria of selection in scarce lifesaving medical resource cases would fail to treat individuals with the respect they deserve.[11] Instead, each person should be seen as having equal claims on these resources based on his or her equal need. To employ other nonmedical criteria is to elevate one person's need over that of another. Since to do so would effectively condemn one person to death, this practice would utterly fail to respect these persons as equals. When two rights of equal weight conflict, we cannot treat the persons fairly by considering less important factors in deciding which right to respect. According to Childress, random criteria at least preserve the equality among persons to which their equal rights claims entitle them. But, this is only true when there is no other relevant basis for distinguishing among these persons which would preserve respect for the values their rights claims are supposed to advance.

Childress has established only that allocation decisions based on irrelevant differences among persons fail to provide concern for equality and dignity. In medicine what should count as a relevant difference among persons, after it has been determined that all candidates do have roughly equal medical need for a scarce resource, is hard to determine. These choices are made all the more difficult by the fact that such medical decisions concern life and death matters. Hence, deciding to employ a certain criterion to refuse treatment to one person is in fact to condemn that person to die. In law, decisions about the allocation of scarce resources rarely have such drastic results. Thus, the decision to employ a certain criterion for refusing legal service to one person who needs it does not necessarily create an irreversible predicament for that individual. For instance, the person denied legal help for his or her divorce in May can reapply in December with considerable but usually not devastating consequences due to the initial denial. This means that allocation schemes in law are not as likely to be all-or-nothing matters as they are when lifesaving medical resources are allocated, and as a result, group-oriented allocation schemes in law are not as likely to be disrespectful of individual dignity as they are in medicine.

Scarce resource allocation in medicine is not properly analogous to that in law, precisely because legal decisions often concern more than one individual person, whereas medical decisions rarely concern treatment which may directly alleviate the suffering of more than one person at a time. As I will next indicate, group-oriented calculations about the allocation of scarce legal resources do not necessarily turn out to be utilitarian calculations. Unlike medicine, a single legal case can meet more than one individual's rights claim. Yet the time spent by an attorney in vindicating ten people's rights claims in one suit will rarely equal that spent in adjudicating ten or even fewer rights claims through individual cases. Thus, consideration of group impact is relevant for legal allocation decisions in ways that it is not for medical decisions.

Maximizing Equal Access

Breger maintains that it is a denial of the right to equal access for poverty law attorneys to decide which cases to take based on social utility or any other consideration that would look to the needs of groups of clients rather than to those of individuals. Consideration of the following three hypothetical cases (based largely on decisions which are commonly made by Legal Services attorneys) will show that Breger's conclusion is implausible even assuming his equal access perspective.

Case 1. Two prospective clients arrive at a Legal Services office each seeking legal counsel. The first person wants a divorce from his or her spouse, while the second wants to challenge the gas company's policy of shutoff following nonpayment of bills. Breger would maintain that it is unfair to allow the poverty lawyer to make the decision of which case to take (assuming that he or she can only take one case). According to him, the party who is turned away can legitimately complain that his or her rights have not been taken seriously as rights, since they have been overridden by the lawyer's utility calculations. If a lottery had been used, or if it could be shown that one person's rights claim was of higher standing than that of the other (perhaps because it was an emergency, while the other claim could wait), or if one person voluntarily decided to step aside in favor of the other, or if all poor persons relegated this kind of decision to a citizen board in advance, then, as Breger would have it, the right to access of one of those persons would not necessarily be infringed. For him, distinguishing cases by subject matter unjustly rewards the rights claim of the others.

Case 2. Eleven prospective clients arrive at a Legal Services office each seeking legal counsel. The first person wants a divorce, while the second, third, fourth, fifth, sixth, seventh, eighth, ninth, tenth, and eleventh clients want to challenge the gas company's shutoff policy. Again the lawyer can only handle one case. Which case should he or she take and what should he or she consider in determining an answer according to Breger's conceptual analysis? Given the fact that the lawyer can provide counsel to ten of the prospective clients by handling any one of the gas company shutoff complaints as a class action suit, and thereby this lawyer can provide access to all ten of these people, it is counterintuitive to maintain that this consideration should not weigh heavily in the lawyer's decision.

If one places access to the legal system high on one's list of goods or values in a society, as Breger surely does, then a decision that provides this good for ten and denies it to one is surely better than a decision that provides it to one and denies it to ten. Or to use rights terminology, handling the gas company case as a class action suit would meet access rights better and deny the smallest number of access rights claims. Even in a universe where only rights claims can legitimately override other rights claims, numbers should count in the sense that the option of providing more rights fulfillment would override the option of providing less rights fulfillment. This conclusion is consistent with Breger's strong emphasis on equal access.

Case 3. Two prospective clients arrive at a Legal Services office each seeking legal counsel. The first person wants a divorce, the second wants to challenge the gas company's shutoff policy. The Legal Services attorney has good reason to believe that at least nine other people in the community also want to change the gas company's policy but have not yet presented themselves to the Legal Services attorney in the office. Should the lawyer disregard the fact that there are at least ten people whose legal needs will be met by handling the gas company suit instead of the divorce? Is it a denial of the right to access of the first person, or is it a justified overriding of his or her right in order to maximize access rights? On Breger's own grounds it is justified, indeed perhaps even required, that the lawyer choose to handle the suit which will provide the greatest fulfillment of access rights. Again, if such a high value is placed on the mere fulfillment of access rights, one need not look to social utility to show that some calculations based on group impact can be justified.

Conceptually, Breger has confused two rather different kinds of calculations. The first is the standard utilitarian calculation that looks only to the preferences or interests of the greatest number of people in attempting to maximize well-being or happiness. The second is the calculation that looks to the rights of individuals but recognizes that these rights are not all unique. This second calculation recognizes that many people or even groups of people may have similar rights claims. It would require, where possible, that such claims be joined in order to maximize the fulfillment of these rights claims, or at lest to minimize their infringement.

Appeals to access rights will not allow Breger to block this second kind of calculation since it maximizes the fulfillment of access rights. Perhaps it could be shown that allowing the rights of many to override the right of one is to treat this one person as not fully human. However, not even Breger contends that each denial of right constitutes disrespect, for he maintains that a right may be respectfully overridden if one can show that a more important right conflicts with it.[12] Rights claims stand high in our universe of moral discourse because rights are thought to protect individuals from being treated as means for the majority's benefit. But not every overriding of rights automatically signals a denial of respect for the person involved. If such denials must occur so that the rights of many are not denied, and if the rights of the many as well as the rights of the one person are of the same type, then it is not disrespectful to deny the right of the one to protect the rights of the many.

Group-Impact Allocations and Rights Theory

Breger maintains throughout his essay that any attempt to allocate legal resources by reference to group impact is a utilitarian calculation which is incompatible with access rights theory.[13] I argue that certain numerical calculations are not incompatible with what is at the basis of rights theory. Rights theory does not require that we disregard the number of individuals whose rights claims are affected in allocation decisions.

Underlying any rights theory is the idea that each person should count for one and only one, that is, that each person should be afforded equal respect — not equal respect when compared with ten other people all also viewed as persons, but equal respect with each other person, each seen simply as one other person. When there are no relevant differences among persons we may flip coins to decide the outcome because doing so gives each person an exactly equal chance of getting the desired outcome. In these cases we have no basis for distinguishing among individuals, and any nonrelevant basis would provide less opportunity to one or another of these persons, thereby failing to treat that person equally to each of the others. But is it true that in all cases the number of people who possess a right is irrelevant?

Consider four persons in a lifeboat: we can either save one person (who needs three gallons of water) or we can save the other three (each of whom needs only one gallon). Assume that there is no morally relevant basis for distinguishing among the four and that each has a right to life which entails that we should do that which is necessary to save each life. That is, each has a right to life and a corresponding right to be saved. But we are in a situation of scarcity — not all can be saved. Either one can be saved and the other three die, or the three can be saved and the one dies. This situation is closer to that facing the Legal Services lawyer, than the medical scenario where only two persons are involved. So that I do not beg the question, also assume that the only thing which is relevant in this case is the right to be saved, and no amount of any social good can override the right for any person. I will argue that, by appealing to the rights theory alone, it is permissible to decide the issue by choosing the greatest number rather than the one person to be saved.

Those who deny this thesis seem to be committed to the following premise: "If one person is harmed, that would be just as bad as if a number are each equally harmed."[14] But what could possibly support such a view? One might claim that the harms of the larger number cannot be summed, that they must be taken and compared with the harm to each, one by one, and in this scenario it would never be justified to pick one over the other.[15] But again, why must we be limited to this nonaggregative view of harms? There is nothing intrinsic to rights theory which rules out all group-oriented allocation procedures.

Perhaps it could be argued that the harm of having a right overridden is a harm of the sort which possesses overwhelming significance regardless of how many persons are so affected. Is this plausible? If we look at it from the perspective of any one person who might be so harmed, it might appear that this is so. Most individuals would not agree to suffer so that others will not have to suffer, and this is surely the case when one's own life is at stake. But how does one explain one's position to the others who each would have suffered? It would appear to the others that their collective suffering, and in the case at hand, their loss of lives, is not worth what the loss of life was worth to the one. To say, for instance, that Jones' suffering is equal to the suffering of three is, from the perspective of the three, to say that the suffering of any of the three is only equal to one-third of Jones' suffering — and this would surely not be to treat each person with equal respect.

Furthermore, if we let the numbers count then we can say that Jones' suffering is not equal to the suffering of the three. Instead, Jones' suffering is equal to only the suffering of one-third of the three (where each suffers equally), and this would seemingly preserve the sense in which we respect each person's suffering or loss of rights equally. The principle should be that no person will be given enough weight to his or her own (equal) suffering so as to override the suffering of more than one. To disallow quantification is to deny the thesis, thought to be essential to rights theory, that each person is to be treated with equal respect. As Derek Parfit quite succinctly puts it: "Why do we save the larger number? Because we do give equal weight to saving each. Each counts for one. That is why more count for more."[16] Only if I were also to allow that individual rights could be overridden by the weaker interests of others would I be vulnerable to the charge that I had slipped from the maximization of rights to the maximization of preferences, and only then would I be vulnerable to the charge that I had not taken rights, and respect for persons, seriously. Looking to the group impact in seeking to minimize the number of those whose rights will be denied is not the kind of utilitarian concern which is incompatible with what has traditionally been the basis for rights theory.

The Benefits of Group-Oriented Decision Making

I have argued that group-oriented case selection procedures and litigation strategies are not inherently inconsistent with a concern for individual rights. The next step is to show briefly how such procedures and strategies perform useful roles in maximizing access, given the nature of much poverty litigation. First, and perhaps most obviously, such group-oriented procedures and strategies are often the most efficient way to vindicate legal rights. Second, group litigation procedures and strategies increase the likelihood that conflicting concerns among the poor, particularly about appropriate remedies, can at least be considered by an adjudicator. Third, the poor have unique common concerns, which give them interests as a group, interests which cannot wholly be protected even through repetitive individual litigation. Finally, many government and other institutional adversaries of the poor treat the poor as a group, and their invidious actions can only be effectively met by strategies which recognize and respond to such group treatment.

The aggregation of rights claims into a single suit may not only maximize the fulfillment of rights claims, but also may be the most efficient way to settle legal disputes between the poor and their opponents. Even equal access proponents, such as Breger, admit that efficiency considerations are relevant "insofar as they have an impact on the quest for procedural justice."[17] Moreover, such proponents do not deny that certain efficiency considerations, e.g., whether the client's claim can succeed,[18] can be used in deciding to whom scarce legal resources should be allocated.

Rule 23 of the Federal Rules of Civil Procedure adopts such efficiency considerations as its primary rationale.[19] The aggregation of individual claims avoids duplication in discovery, pleading, and trial preparation. Rule 23 not only permits a saving of judicial resources, but also allows attorneys to save time by litigating a case on behalf of a class rather than trying each case separately. The resulting savings in attorney time can, in the Legal Services context, rebound to the benefit of those clients who would not otherwise be served because they requested or needed services after the program's capacity at any particular time had been reached.

Furthermore, many recent civil rights cases have illustrated that group litigation is the only means to ensure an appropriate legal remedy for certain kinds of harm. Poor people's problems often result from institutional unresponsiveness. The poor are generally dependent on governmental agencies for many of their basic needs such as welfare, medical care, and public housing. The poor, more often than the nonpoor, are also engaged in legal disputes with institutions such as nursing homes, mental health facilities, and housing corporations. But if the suits are handled as individual cases, evidentiary considerations limit the framework for the court's decisions, and precedent circumscribes the scope of relief which the court may order to vindicate an individual's claim. Often, such relief is retrospective only, even when realistically speaking, the illegal practices are bound to recur.

Second, even though somewhat limited, the precedential impact of an individual lawsuit may affect the interests of other poor persons who are not heard in the suit. Recent class action litigation has demonstrated that a narrow definition of the plaintiff class may exclude participation of people who have legitimate interests in the outcome of the suit. Such litigation may artificially restrict the facts and remedies which the court may consider in framing relief. For instance, in *Halderman* v. *Pennhurst State School & Hospital*, conditions in a Pennsylvania institution for the mentally retarded were challenged.[20] The use of a narrow definition of the class, to include only institutionalized individuals and their guardians *ad litem*, resulted in a sweeping judicial remedy which effectively closed down the Pennhurst facility.[21] This remedy was later challenged by parents not consulted in the original case, who claimed to be injured because their children could no longer remain in Pennhurst.[22] Similarly, individual litigation such as *Regents of the University of California* v. *Bakke* may cause the reordering of legal relationships of many who cannot, for one reason or the other, establish their right to different treatment based on their individual circumstances.[23] This is particularly problematical because the poor generally lack funding to vindicate their rights to different treatment by distinguishing their own situations.

Third, the poor have common economic interests which are often in jeopardy in civil suits. Such common interests result from the unique difficulty which the poor have in meeting their minimum needs. It is surely true that the "package" of what counts as minimum needs is not the same from society to society or from time to time.[24] But such variations do not indicate that the poor in any given society do not have a common interest in meeting their needs. For instance, in advanced societies where electricity and natural gas for heating are considered minimum needs, the poor, like everyone else, must pay more for these services when utility rates increase. Unlike all other persons, however, the poor must dip into money reserved for other minimum needs in order to pay for the increase in utility costs, or go without electricity or heat. All members of a society have some interest in the price of providing for their minimal needs. Yet the poor have a uniquely pressing interest in these matters since they can pay for these increases only by going without other minimum needs.

The common interests of the poor create a situation in which group impact litigation will have at least an indirect effect on all of the poor in a given region. Thus, any conflict that might exist between the interests of an individual who has been turned down for legal services and the interests of the group who will be made the object of a class action suit is somewhat mitigated. The poor person who is turned down for service in a pending divorce is quite likely to be benefitted by a group-oriented case which seeks to challenge utility rate increases. While it is true that the divorce may be more important to that person than the rate increase, it is nonetheless true that his or her interests, which include an interest in the rate increase, are not strictly in conflict with the interests of the people who want to challenge the utility rate increase through a class action.

The poor also face problems which, considered from the perspective of any given poor person, appear insufficient to warrant litigation, but which have a clearly adverse impact when considered collectively. Think of the decision not to construct a public housing project in a certain neighborhood. Such a decision may have a severe adverse effect on all residents in the neighborhood. But if we focus merely on individual harm, such that we are concerned in a given case only with the effects of the decision on one member of this community, then the harm is not the sort that seems likely to be taken seriously by a judge. It is very difficult to prove that a given poor person would have been eligible to get into a public housing complex, and what harm that person suffered because he or she now is not in that complex. The harm, though, is easily recognizable when the whole group of neighbors is considered. Without the new housing complex, overcrowding and inadequate housing create difficulties for every member of the neighborhood; and ancillary problems of crime and sanitation, common to overcrowded areas, emerge.

In similar ways, the unresolved legal problems of the poor perpetuate and contribute to poverty in America. But poverty itself is hard to understand as the plight of isolated individuals and it is even more difficult to remedy. When individual suits are filed, defendants commonly try to settle out of court. These settlements often effectively pay off the individual poor person, but leave the cause of the problem untouched for the individual and most especially for others similarly situated. This is the other side of the problem of precedent. Out-of-court settlements do not even afford the slight relief that court-supervised settlements, through the doctrine of precedent, offer to those unnamed in the suit.

Finally, the poor more often than the nonpoor face institutional opponents in legal proceedings.[25] These institutional opponents tend to view the poor as a class. In this context, think of the food stamp program. The regulations promulgated affect every person whose income is under the federal poverty line. If a decision is made to lower eligibility standards, then every person who falls between the old eligibility line and the new line, regardless of differences in individual situations, is affected by that decision. A class is created by the actions of the food stamp director. It is true that not all of the poor are here treated as a class, but the institutional opponent has categorized situations in such a way that individual poor persons are not distinguished except according to overly broad characteristics such as income.

The actions of the institutional officials in creating classes of poor individuals require appropriate response from the legal system. Such response cannot be made by characterizing adjudication according to an individualistic conception of law. Civil lawsuits are often characterized, especially by individualists who are also rights theorists, as involving essentially private disputes between discrete, individual plaintiffs and defendants.[26] Appeal to law is merely one of many ways that individuals may attempt to settle their problems. The law enters, according to this view, only as a third party to the conflict between these private parties.

However, when the parties in a case are an institution and the class it has created, then the adjudication problem facing a judge is as much a political problem as a problem of dispute resolution. In class action suits the named plaintiff is merely a representative member of an aggrieved group. Class action suits explicitly recognize that institutional actions create a pattern of treatment for a group of individuals. From the earliest use of this type of suit, the interest which serves to constitute the group of litigants has been their social status, something which could not be understood by reference to the individual members of the group *qua* individuals.[27]

A group of poor tenants residing in a public housing project may be said to have a similar economic status, defined by their dependence on the public housing authority, which creates problems of status rather than of rights for the members as a group. By contrast, when litigation is brought in behalf of all antibiotic purchasers, they are regarded as a class only for convenience; they could be viewed as individuals with similar problems without any loss of conceptual understanding of their legal problems. Yet, the class designation of the members of the public housing project is not merely one which originates in convenience.

The welfare official or public housing administrator does not promulgate a regulation or take action based on information about its effects on each and every poor person within the ambit of a program. Rather the official weighs considerations of the poor tenants ·as a homogeneous group against public concerns such as saving money, in order to implement sweeping changes that have an equal impact on all members. The benefits and burdens which such an official distributes are proffered in identical ways to each member of the group, based solely on his or her membership in the group of the poor, and not by individually considering whether any particular member of the group should have received those benefits and burdens. These actions violate the dictates of, or purposes behind, laws passed to aid the poor as a group. In such circumstances, only legal responses which recognize the poor as a group will sufficiently guard the interests of all members.

Class action litigation represents the most effective way to represent the legal interests of the group as a whole. In the public housing example, the class action will aid in establishing how the group-oriented perspective of the housing authority has visited harms on some individuals, and is likely to do so on others, because of broadened discovery and proof rules. By allowing the court to remedy not only past injuries but also contemplated injuries to members of the group, the class action device goes beyond the scope of the individual lawsuit, in which rights and remedies flow only between individual persons who have caused or suffered specific harms. In this way the class action suit can benefit poor individuals by having an impact on the chief problem facing the poor as a group — their poverty — and thereby secure the rights of the greatest number of poor persons. Such strategies are consistent with the dictates of justice when group-based harms have occurred, especially to unorganized social groups.

II. Organized Groups and Disadvantaged Individuals

One of the most difficult criticisms faced by the analysis I have offered is that the permissibility of restricting the speech of for-profit corporations may sweep so far as to render permissible state restrictions on the speech of corporations which are established expressly to promote the rights of those who are disadvantaged or even disenfranchised. A corporation such as the NAACP, then, may find that it can be legitimately restricted from various exercises of free speech and association by states which happen to disagree with its objectives. My position on the *Bellotti* case (in chapter six) may then be seen to be at odds with what I have so far argued in chapter seven, since I have argued that it is appropriate and sometimes even required that group-oriented strategies be adopted when there has been significant disadvantage to a large group. In this section I will argue that my position on the *Bellotti* case is not excessively sweeping. Indeed, the court decisions on the rights of the NAACP have already set the stage for distinguishing between organized social groups based on the purposes they serve.

In *NAACP* v. *Alabama* (1958), the Supreme Court held that the NAACP could sue on behalf of its members' first amendment rights, but it left open the question of whether the Association itself had first amendment rights. Writing for the majority, Justice Harlan wrote:

> We think that petitioner argues more appropriately the rights of its members, and that its nexus with them is sufficient to permit that it acts as their representative before this Court. . . . The Association . . . is but the medium through which its individual members seek to make more effective the expression of their own views.[28]

Furthermore, the Court said that while it did not matter whether the beliefs of the members were political, economic, or religious,[29] the rights in question were especially important "where the group espouses dissident beliefs."[30]

Five years later in *NAACP* v. *Button* (1963) Justice Brennan made a distinction between types of corporation the centerpiece of his decision for the majority.

> We think petitioner may assert this right on its own behalf, because, though a corporation, it is directly engaged in those activities claimed to be constitutionally protected, which the state would curtail. . . . Groups which find themselves unable to achieve their objective through the ballot frequently turn to the courts. . . . And under the conditions of modern government, litigation may well be the sole practicable avenue open to a minority to petition for its grievances. . . . The NAACP is not a conventional political party; but the litigation it assists, while serving to vindicate the rights of members of the American Negro community, at the same time, and perhaps more importantly, makes possible the distinctive contribution of a minority group to the ideas and beliefs of our society.[31]

And while Brennan admitted that the substance of the beliefs in question was irrelevant,[32] and even that the social utility of those beliefs was irrelevant,[33] it did matter that the group had difficulty making these beliefs known due to the disadvantaged status of its members. This was seen most clearly when in both NAACP cases, the Supreme Court rejected arguments presented by the states of Alabama and Virginia attempting to apply the Court's earlier rejection of putatively similar rights of expression by the Ku Klux Klan. While the Court was willing to support just as strongly those *individuals* who would "arouse our society against the objectives of the petitioner,"[34] *group* protection seemed to be tied to the express purposes of the organization, that is, in the case of the NAACP, to the promotion of speakers who would not otherwise be heard because of their disadvantaged status.

I believe that the Court was on the right track in the *NAACP* cases in drawing a distinction between those organized groups that are deserving of special legal protection and those that are not. It is not that corporations are similar to individual humans that makes some of them deserving of the kind of legal protection afforded individual humans. Rather it is the way that certain corporations do or do not advance the interests of already disadvantaged individuals that counts in assessing whether these corporations are themselves deserving of special legal protection. Legal protection may be afforded, in some cases, even when this protection is purchased at the expense of the interests or rights of select individuals, such as is true whenever a group such as the NAACP is given protection at the expense of the interests of racist individuals.

In the remainder of this section, I will provide an argument in support of the above outlined position by showing that the purposes of an organized group in protecting or advancing the interests of disadvantaged individuals should warrant special legal protection for such groups, even where the rights of some individuals may be harmed by this special legal protection. I wish to defend three claims. First, groups of disadvantaged persons should have a legal priority over persons who are not disadvantaged. Second, group-oriented legal and political strategies are more effective in securing the interests and rights of disadvantaged persons than are individually oriented strategies. Finally, organized groups which do not have the interests of the disadvantaged as their goals should be excluded from this special protection.

In the Anglo-American system of jurisprudence, the disputants in a legal action are presumed to stand before the court on equal footing. But such a presumption is not justified when members of a disadvantaged group face legal opponents who are not from a similarly disadvantaged group. Economically or politically disadvantaged litigants are legally disadvantaged in at least two ways. First, the members of a disadvantaged group are more at risk than other litigants in that their marginal economic or political position makes them greater potential losers in civil suits. In the case of economically disadvantaged group members, monetary damages mean loss of the means to provide basic necessities. In the case of politically disadvantaged group members, adverse court decisions are less likely to be successfully challenged through the legislative process. Second, all successful litigation depends on zealous counsel and fair judicial officials. Economically disadvantaged group members are much less likely to be able to afford the kind of zealous legal counsel that others in the population can afford. And politically disadvantaged group members are much less likely to find unbiased and sympathetic judges and juries than are those litigants who come from the political mainstream of American society.

Since economically and politically disadvantaged group members do not approach the courts on an equal footing to those who are not so disadvantaged, they deserve special legal protection. This special protection is justified through the goal of the legal system itself, namely, to provide dispute resolution procedures which do not favor one party over the other. When the procedures work to the advantage of already advantaged members of a community, then the presumption of "equality before the law" is not justified, and a corrective measure is needed to bring the legal procedures back to fairness.

For most disadvantaged individuals, the best corrective measures at law provide a priority to the collective interests of discrete groups of disadvantaged individuals. The reasons for this are many, and some were mentioned earlier in this chapter. Here it will be helpful to elaborate upon the reasons which the Supreme Court gave in the *NAACP* cases. When individuals are poor and politically under-represented, it is incumbant on these individuals to combine or pool whatever limited resources they may have and seek to achieve their goals collectively. As far as free speech is concerned, the better or-ganized a group of poor persons becomes the more likely it is that its collective voice will be heard. Those who are poor and Black have historically been in the worst position for achieving effective liberty in America; and this group is most in need of a corporate body like the NAACP to speak in behalf of the interests of this group, both on the political stage and before the courts.[35] The Supreme Court recognized just this fact in its landmark decisions in 1958 and 1963.

What the Court recognized was that few if any poor Blacks would be able effectively to achieve protection of their civil liberties if these Blacks were not collectively represented by a lobbying group such as the NAACP. And to offset the legal disadvantage that comes from economic disadvantage, the Courts gave the NAACP a special status, one different from other corporations. The Court allowed the NAACP to have the legal rights to speech normally afforded only to human individuals. The NAACP was granted this status because of the be-lief that it constituted the most effective speaker in behalf of all poor Blacks in America. This rationale is quite different, and I believe much more defensible, than that provided over twenty years later when the

Supreme Court granted The First National Bank of Boston free speech rights as well.

Organized groups like The First National Bank of Boston should not be granted the status of rights-bearer that a group like the NAACP has been granted. In the *Bellotti* case, the majority of the Supreme Court contended that corporations resembled individual human persons sufficiently to warrant granting them free speech rights. In the *NAACP* cases, the Court contended that when there is a sufficient nexus between an organized group and its members, then that group can be regarded as the repository of the aggregated rights of its members. That is not to say, on the basis of the *NAACP* cases, that the group should be seen as having rights itself, but only that by granting certain rights to the group the useful purpose of protecting the aggregated rights of its members is served. The *Bellotti* opinion goes much further than the defensible position of the *NAACP* cases. *Bellotti* stands for the view that social groups are entities with rights of their own, a view which I have been disputing throughout the previous chapters.

When questions of distributive justice arise, and groups are involved, one should look to the relative degree of disadvantage of the members of the group. If the members are not relatively disadvantaged, then the claims of the group should be given no priority over the claims of individuals. If the members are relatively disadvantaged, then it may be possible to make a case for a special legal or moral status for the group. The analysis must oscilate between individuals and groups; we cannot remain merely at the level of groups in order to answer basic questions of distributive justice. The status of groups with respect to the issue of justice cannot be determined independently of the degree of disadvantage of the individuals who are and are not members of the groups in question. Once again, it seems to me that there is good reason to reject both individualism and the view that social groups are entities or persons in their own right. In deliberations about justice, as with many moral issues, a middle position turns out to be the most fruitful.

Conclusion

The previous discussion of the moral status of social groups has been concerned with two distinct topics: those moral concepts used to assess the intentional actions taken by a group, and those moral concepts used to assess the harms done to a group. In the first part (chapters one to four), I argued that many social groups which lacked tight organizational structures could be said to be collectively responsible for the joint actions of their members. And in the second part (chapters five to seven), I argued that still more social groups — more than those that were capable of engaging in joint action — are capable of being harmed. Throughout, I have emphasized how conceptualizing social groups in moral terms best makes sense of various social phenomena.

Chapter one argued that the structure of a social group could be best understood in terms of the relationships that exist among the members of a group. I contended that understanding this structure does not require that we posit the independent existence of the social group. But I also claimed that it is not sufficient merely to speak of the psychological states of individual members in order to give a full explanation of group structure. Reference must be made to something social. As a result, a third alternative model was proposed for understanding social groups, namely, the view of groups as individuals *in* relationships.

Throughout the remainder of the book I tried to defend the view of chapter one by showing that in case after case the two reigning views of social groups, variously called collectivism and individualism, were inadequate. This inadequacy revealed itself most clearly in the chapters on collective action (chapter two) and group interest (chapter five). I will spend the next few paragraphs on these topics before turning to the more general conclusions that can be drawn from the entire discussion so far.

In chapters two and three, I defended a view espoused by Jean-Paul Sartre on the status of unorganized groups, such as mobs, and I elaborated my view about the status of organized groups through the moral concepts of action and intent. The analysis of mob behavior showed that such factors as solidarity cannot be explained by reference to individual psychological motivations and may operate as efficient motivators even in large mobs. And the discussion in chapter five went on to show that collective interest in unorganized groups does not depend even on the awareness of the individual members that they are members of a given group. A middle position on the status of social groups was proposed and shown to be the most plausible. In unorganized groups, solidarity and other relationships allow the group to have action and interest even though no decision-making structure for the group exists, contrary to what collectivists have claimed. And these relationships also prevent the reduction of the group's action and interest to the aggregate actions and interests of the individual members, contrary to what individualists have claimed.

In the Introduction I referred to the essay "Justice as Fairness" in which John Rawls says that the term "person" encompasses not only human individuals but also "nations, provinces, business firms, churches, teams, and so on." In *A Theory of Justice*, Rawls says at the beginning that justice may function differently for human individuals than for social groups,[1] but later he continues his earlier practice of talking of persons as either "human individuals or associations."[2] Rawls is paradigmatic of most of moral philosophy in that he fails to examine carefully the differences that exist between individuals and groups.

In general, I have argued that moral theorists need to examine more closely the actions and interests of social groups. Such an examination will provide a much richer understanding of the variety of experiences to which moral concepts are applied. And this means that the understanding of concepts such as "responsibility," "rights," and "justice" should be adjusted to fit cases which do not involve merely isolated individual actors and actions.

The concepts of justice and responsibility are handed down to us from an age when the isolated individual was not in center stage. For the Greeks, justice concerned proportionality, that is, with giving each person his or her due according to the roles and positions which those people occupied in a given society. This conception of justice, while forcing us to look at each individual person's merits, is equally concerned with the social milieu, and could not plausibly be understood in abstraction from that milieu.[3] In the Middle Ages, the concept of responsibility was group-oriented as well. In Germanic tribal and feudal societies, moral and legal responsibility was understood as the response that the members of one group owed to another group for the harm perpetrated by one of its members upon a member of the other group. Personal responsibility only made sense after the question of group responsibility had been answered.[4]

It has become commonplace today not to take seriously these older moral concepts, in the same way that it has become common to abandon ancient scientific concepts. But surely these moral conceptions are worth reconsideration especially since larger social units are again at center stage of contemporary experience. Few, if any, individuals are self-sufficient, and no person fails to be a member of at least one social group. No one is unaffected by the actions of corporations, majority parties, and professional associations. Hence, contemporary moral theorists should be at least as concerned with social groups as were the Ancients.

When social groups are evaluated in moral terms it is difficult to resist the temptation to reduce such group evaluation to individual evaluation. I have suggested that this strategy makes the most sense in the case of rights ascriptions. It is, again, no coincidence that rights theory is unique to the modern age and arose in an individualistic era. Rights theorists continue to accentuate the tradition of viewing the moral and legal concepts of rights as protecting individuals from the unwarranted intrusions of groups and other individuals. I can find no fault with this strategy. But I do not believe that rights theory should serve as the model for our concepts of justice and responsibility, as has been suggested by various libertarian theorists.[5] Justice and responsibility can function differently in moral assessments than individualistically oriented rights can. Responsibility can be applied to the assessment of relationships and roles within both formally organized and unorganized groups of individual persons. And justice can be applied to the relative status of these groups when compared to one another. In both cases, the evaluation of a group in moral terms will not necessarily result in a similar assessment of the individual members of the group. It is a mistake not to realize that this is part of the proper domain of justice and responsibility.

Considerations of responsibility and justice are not exhausted by merely looking to discrete individual behavior and harm. Similarly, legal and political strategies which are directed to blame, punishment, and compensation should not be restricted to the domain of individuals either. In both theory and practice, social groups must be taken into account. Our explanations as well as our social and legal practices need to be adjusted to the increasing role that these social groups play in ordinary moral experience. Discussions of collective responsibility and justice for groups should be brought to center stage in ethics. If this book aids in that effort, it will have succeeded.

Notes

INTRODUCTION

1. Larry May and John C. Hughes, "Sexual Harassment," *Social Theory and Practice* 6 (Fall 1980): pp. 249–280.

2. See John Rawls, "Justice as Fairness," *Philosophical Review* (1955): pp. 164–194, reprinted in W. Sellars and J. Hospers, eds., *Readings in Ethical Theory* (Englewood Cliffs, N.J.: Prentice-Hall, 1970), p. 579.

3. Jean-Paul Sartre, *Critique of Dialectical Reason*, trans. Alan Sheridan-Smith, (London: Verso/NLB, 1976 [1960]).

1. THE NATURE OF SOCIAL GROUPS

1. Lon Fuller, *Legal Fictions* (Stanford, Calif.: Stanford University Press, 1967), p. 1.

2. Ibid., pp. 12–13.

3. See ibid., p. 22.

4. Ibid., p. 117.

5. Ibid., p. 115.

6. Ibid., pp. 117–118.

7. Rod Bertolet, "Reference, Fiction, and Fictions," *Synthese* 60 (1984): p. 433.

8. J. W. N. Watkins, "Ideal Types and Historical Explanation," in *The Philosophy of Social Explanation*, ed. Alan Ryan (Oxford: Oxford University Press, 1973), p. 88.

9. J. W. N. Watkins, "Methodologial Individualism and Social Tendencies," reprinted in *Readings in the Philosophy of Social Science*, ed. May Brodbeck (New York: Macmillan Co. 1968), pp. 270–271.

10. Watkins, "Ideal Types," p. 104.

11. See May Brodbeck, "Methodological Individualisms: Definition and Reduction," reprinted in *Readings in the Philosophy of the Social Sciences*, ed. May Brodbeck (New York: Macmillan Co., 1968), pp. 284–286.

12. Emile Durkheim, *The Rules of Sociological Method*, trans. S. Solovay and J. Mueller, ed. Catlin (New York: Free Press, 1964 [1895]), p. 7.

13. Ibid., p. 1.

14. Ibid., p. 6.

15. Ibid., p. 7.

16. Emile Durkheim, *The Division of Labor in Society*, trans. W. D. Halls (New York: Free Press, 1984 [1893]), p. 3.

17. See Maurice Mandelbaum, "Societal Facts," in *The Philosophy of Social Explanation*, ed. Alan Ryan (Oxford: Oxford University Press, 1973), pp. 108-110.

18. Peter French, *Collective and Corporate Responsibility* (New York: Columbia University Press, 1984).

19. Ibid., pp. 5 and 13.

20. Ibid., p. 5.

21. Ibid., p. 29.

22. Ibid., p. 27.

23. Ibid., pp. 12-13.

24. See Anthony Quinton, "Social Objects," *Proceedings of the Aristotelian Society, 1975-1976*, pp. 10-11.

25. See David Hillel-Ruben, "The Existence of Social Objects," *Philosophical Quarterly* 32 (October 1982).

26. Richard De George, "Social Reality and Social Relations," *The Review of Metaphysics* 37 (September 1983): p. 3.

27. Ibid., p. 8.

28. Ibid., p. 12.

29. David Copp, "What Collectives Are: Agency, Individualism and Legal Theory," *Dialogue* 23 (1984): pp. 253 and 258; also see "Collective Actions and Secondary Actions," *American Philosophical Quarterly* 16 (July 1979): pp. 177-186.

30. Copp, "What Collectives Are," p. 256.

31. Ibid., p. 252.

32. David Copp, "Hobbes on Artificial Persons and Collective Actions," *The Philosophical Review* 89 (October 1980): p. 604; David Ozar makes a similar point in his paper, "Three Models of Group Choice," *The Journal of Medicine and Philosophy* 7 (1982): pp. 28-29.

2. COLLECTIVE ACTION

1. For a representative selection of views on this subject, see Peter A. French, ed., *Individual and Collective Responsibility: The Massacre at My Lai* (Cambridge, Mass.: Schenkman Publishing Co., 1972).

2. J. W. N. Watkins, "Methodological Individualism and Social Tendencies," p. 273. Watkins allows this counter-example to stand since it seems to depend on a "physical short-circuiting" of the normal thought processes of individual persons.

3. Peter French, *Collective and Corporate Responsibility*, chap. 2.

4. David Copp argues that Hobbes recognized that in certain circumstances "a unanimity condition would otherwise underwrite our assignment of choices and actions to multitudes . . . such as perhaps in the case of the storming of the Bastille by the Paris mob." David Copp, "Hobbes on Artificial Persons," pp. 604-605. Also see his more recent paper, "What Collectives Are," pp. 249-269.

5. For a quite different defense of the claim that Sartre held the view of groups that I attribute to him, see Thomas R. Flynn, *Sartre and Marxist Existentialism*, (Chicago: University of Chicago Press, 1984), especially chapters 6 and 7.

6. Jean-Paul Sartre, *Critique of Dialectical Reason*, pp. 353, 351, 354, 355, 357.

7. For a very different understanding of the concept of solidarity, see Joel Feinberg's essay "Collective Responsibility," *Journal of Philosophy* 65 (1968), reprinted in his book *Doing and Deserving* (Princeton, N.J.: Princeton University Press, 1970).

8. P. S. Atiyah, *Vicarious Liability and the Law of Torts* (London: Butterworths, 1967), p. 382.

9. Peter A. French, "Corporate Moral Agency," in T. Beauchamp and N. Bowie, eds., *Ethical Theory and Business* (Englewood Cliffs, N.J.: Prentice-Hall, 1979), p. 176, revised in *Collective and Corporate Responsibility* (New York: Columbia University Press, 1984), p. 41.

10. Ibid., p. 177.

11. Alvin Goldman, *A Theory of Human Action* (Princeton, N.J.: Princeton University Press, 1970), p. 82.

12. French, "Corporate Moral Agency."

13. John Ladd, "Morality and the Ideal of Rationality in Formal Organizations," reprinted in T. Donaldson and P. Werhane, eds., *Ethical Issues in Business* (Englewood Cliffs, N.J.: Prentice-Hall, Inc., 1979), p. 105.

14. Ibid., p. 110.

15. For this definition the dictionary cites the case of *Dartmouth College* v. *Woodward*, 17 U.S. (4 Wheat.) 518, 636, 657 and *U.S.* v. *Trinidad Coal Co.*, 137 U.S. 160.

16. Contrary to what some have held, see Anthony Quinton, "Social Objects," pp. 5 and 10.

17. I will cite the pages of the Supreme Court opinion in parentheses within the text. For a very interesting opinion on the case, see brief of Adolph J. Ackerman, *amicus curiae*, *American Society of Mechanical Engineers* v. *Hydrolevel Corporation*, October 1981, No. 80–1765, pp. 7–8.

18. On this point, see Virginia Held, "Can a Random Collection of Individuals be Morally Responsible?" *The Journal of Philosophy* 67 (July 23, 1970); and Peter French, "Types of Collectivity and Blame," *The Personalist* 56 (Spring 1975), revised in *Collective and Corporate Responsibility* (New York: Columbia University Press, 1984), chap. 1.

19. Thomas Hobbes, *Leviathan*, chaps. 14–16.

20. Rom Harré, *Social Being* (Totowa, N.J.: Littlefield, Adams and Co., 1980), p. 10.

21. On this point, see David Londley, "On the Actions of Teams," *Inquiry* 21 (1978): pp. 213–218, where an argument is advanced for a similar thesis about the actions of sports teams.

3. COLLECTIVE INTENT

1. See George Rude, *The Crowd in the French Revolution* (Oxford: Clarendon Press, 1959), especially chaps. 4 and 14.

2. Jean-Paul Sartre, *Critique of Dialectical Reason*, p. 372.

3. Ibid., pp. 372–373.

4. Ibid., p. 369.

5. Ibid.

6. Jean-Paul Sartre, *The Emotions: Outline of a Theory*, trans. Bernard Frechtman

(New York: Philosophical Library, 1948), p. 60. Here and elsewhere I have changed the translation from unreflective to pre-reflective as is common in contemporary Sartre scholarship.

7. Virginia Blankenship, "The Dynamics of Intention," in Michael Frese and John Sabini, eds., *Goal Directed Behavior: The Concept of Action in Psychology* (Hillsdale, N.J.: Lawrence Earl Baum Associates, 1985), p. 169.

8. Jean-Paul Sartre, *The Transcendence of the Ego: An Existentialist Theory of Consciousness*, trans. Forrest Williams and Robert Kirkpatrick (New York: Farrar, Straus, and Giroux, 1957), p. 58. Sartre also extends this analysis to groups such as the mob that stormed the Bastille in Paris in 1789 in his book *Critique of Dialectical Reason*, pp. 351-373, especially p. 369.

9. Max Weber, *The Theory of Social and Economic Organization*, trans. A. M. Henderson and Talcott Parsons (New York: Oxford University Press, 1947), p. 136.

10. Emile Durkheim, *The Division of Labor in Society*, trans. W. D. Halls (New York: Free Press, 1984 [1893]), pp. 83-85.

11. Ibid., p. 101.

12. Michael Brown and Amy Goldin, *Collective Behavior* (Palisades, Calif.: Goodyear Publishing Co., 1973), p. 205.

13. Jean-Paul Sartre, *Critique of Dialectical Reason*, p. 369.

14. Brown and Goldin, *Collective Behavior*, p. 206.

15. Joseph B. Tamney, *Solidarity in the Slum* (New York: John Wiley and Sons, 1975), p. 2.

16. See, for example, Daryl J. Bem, Michael A. Wallach, and Nathan Kogan, "Group Decision Making Under Risk Aversive Consequences," *Journal of Personality and Social Psychology* 1 (1965): p. 453.

17. These studies are summarized in "The Desire for Group Achievement," chap. 4. of Alvin Zander's *Motives and Goals in Groups* (New York: Academic Press, 1971), see especially pp. 52-54.

18. Reported in Wolfgang Schonflug, "Goal Directed Behavior as a Source of Stress: Psychological Origins and Consequences of Inefficiency," in Frese and Sabini, eds., *Goal Directed Behavior*, (Hillsdale, N.J.: Lawrence Earl Baum Associates, 1985), p. 182.

19. I have borrowed this analogy from Richard De George, "Social Reality and Social Relations," p. 13.

20. Chris Argyris and Donald Schon, *Organizational Learning: A Theory of Action Perspective*, (Andover, Mass.: Addison-Wesley Publishing Co., 1978), pp. 19-20.

21. Gordon Donaldson and Jay W. Lorsch, *Decision Making at the Top: The Shaping of Strategic Decision* (New York: Basic Books, 1983), pp. 81-82.

22. Ibid.

23. David J. Hickson, Richard J. Butler, David Cray, Geoffrey R. Mallory, and David C. Wilson, "Comparing 150 Decision Processes," in Johannes M. Pennings and Associates, ed., *Organizational Strategy and Change* (San Francisco, Calif.: Jossey-Bass Publishers, 1985), p. 140.

24. Peter French, *Collective and Corporate Responsibility*, p. 39.

25. Ibid., p. 47.

26. Ibid., p. 41.

27. Ibid., p. 42 and elsewhere.

28. For a more detailed argument, see Larry May, "Vicarious Agency and Corporate Responsibility," *Philosophical Studies* (1983): pp. 70–72.

29. Thomas Donaldson, *Corporations and Morality* (Englewood Cliffs, N.J.: Prentice-Hall, Inc., 1982), p. 22.

30. French, *Collective and Corporate Responsibility*, pp. 165–166.

4. COLLECTIVE RESPONSIBILITY

1. See, for example, H. D. Lewis, "Collective Responsibility," *Philosophy* 23 (1948).

2. See Hannah Arendt's book *Eichmann in Jerusalem* (New York: Viking, 1963) and the wide variety of popular and scholarly attempts to refute her analysis of collective responsibility.

3. See the first few volumes of the journals *Philosophy and Public Affairs* and *Social Theory and Practice*, both of which were founded to give philosophers a forum for writing about the Vietnam war and other current social and political events. Also see Joel Feinberg's 1968 essay "Collective Responsibility," reprinted as chap. 9 of *Doing and Deserving*.

4. Peter A. French, *Individual and Collective Responsibility: The Massacre at My Lai*.

5. See for example, Peter French, *Collective and Corporate Responsibility*. An awareness of the problem of seemingly unorganized, and often violent, actions taken by groups of persons has not disappeared. I quote from our local paper from the fall of 1984:

> Purdue University officials said they will wait to discipline students who participated in this weekend's off-campus uprising until fragments of the incident are pieced together. All that remained last night from the incident in which 21 people were arrested was the damage to businesses and cars—and obscenities spray painted on State Street. Approximately 1,000 college-age youths were involved in the disturbance, which began at 11:59 p.m. Friday. Joseph L. Bennett, director of Purdue's Office of Public Information, said Saturday that university officials would have to wait until the first of the week before the investigation could be completed. "It will be difficult to take blanket action unless there is an identifiable group involved," he said. (*The Lafayette Journal and Courier*, Monday, October 8, 1984, p. 1.)

6. W. J. H. Sprott, *Human Groups* (New York: Penguin, 1958), pp. 160–161.

7. Alvin I. Goldman, "Toward a Theory of Social Power," *Philosophical Studies* 23 (1972): pp. 234–241. Also see Peter French's attempt to apply Goldman's analysis to cases of crowds and corporations, chap. 5 of his recent book *Collective and Corporate Responsibility*.

8. H. L. A. Hart and A. M. Honoré, *Causation in the Law* (Oxford: Clarendon Press, 1959).

9. Ibid., p. 179.

10. For a more detailed discussion, see Larry May, "Professional Action and the Liabilities of Professional Associations," *Business and Professional Ethics Journal* 2 (Fall 1982): pp. 5–9.

11. Harper Lee, *To Kill a Mockingbird* (New York: Lippincott, 1960), p. 168.

12. Gustav Le Bon, *The Crowd: A Study of the Popular Mind* (T. Fisher Unwin, Ltd., 1896), p. 34. Also see Watkins, "Methodological Individualism and Social Tendencies," p. 273.

13. Of course some philosophers would claim that these bystanders have a responsibility to prevent harm, but this is a general responsibility that each of us has, as humans, to prevent harm where we can. I am talking, though, about special responsibilities which result from what one has done, rather than from being human generally.

14. Lewis, "Collective Responsibility," p. 3.

15. Joel Feinberg, "Collective Responsibility," p. 223.

16. For a quite different view of how a Sartrian understanding of collective responsibility fits Feinberg's categories, see Thomas Flynn, *Sartre and Marxist Existentialism* (Chicago: University of Chicago Press, 1984), p. 181.

17. See Joel Feinberg's excellent summary of the theory of vicarious liability employed in legal theory, "Collective Responsibility," pp. 229–233.

18. See Larry May and John C. Hughes "Coercion in the Workplace," in *Moral Rights in the Workplace*, ed. Gertrude Ezorski (Albany, N.Y.: State University of New York Press, 1987), pp. 115–122.

19. For a detailed examination of numerous real cases from which this composite was drawn, see Larry May and John C. Hughes, "Sexual Harassment," *Social Theory and Practice* 6 (Fall 1980): pp. 249–280.

20. John Ladd, "Morality and the Ideal of Rationality in Formal Organizations," reprinted in Thomas Donaldson and Patricia Werhane, eds., *Ethical Issues in Business* (Englewood Cliffs, N.J.: Prentice-Hall), p. 110.

21. *U.S.* v. *Park*, 421 U.S. 658, 95 S. Ct. 1903 (1975). A more recent case involved the conviction of high-ranking officers of a corporation for manslaughter in the death of a worker exposed to hydrogen cyanide in a film processing plant. See *The New York Times*, June 15, 1985, pp. 1 and 9.

22. 421 U.S. 660, 95 S. Ct. 1906.

23. 421 U.S. 664–665, 95 S. Ct. 1907–1908.

24. 421 U.S. 671, 95 S. Ct. 1911.

25. 421 U.S. 674, 95 S. Ct. 1912.

26. 421 U.S. 679, 95 S. Ct. 1915. The dissent disagreed only with the jury instruction, which did not make it sufficiently clear that Park had to be shown to have been negligent to be liable for the crime.

27. Larry May, "Vicarious Agency and Corporate Responsibility," *Philosophical Studies*, 43 (1983): pp. 69–82.

28. Joel Feinberg, "Collective Responsibility," p. 245.

29. For a contrasting view of the relevance of conspiracies to corporate responsibility, see Joseph S. Ellin, "The Justice of Collective Responsibility," *University of Dayton Review* 15 (Winter 1981–82): pp. 17–28.

30. *State* v. *Burns*, 215 Minn. 182, 187, 9 N.W. 2d 518, 520–1 (1943) cited in Rollin M. Perkins, *Criminal Law*, 2d ed. (Mineola, N.Y.: The Foundation Press, 1969), p. 637.

31. *Moreland* v. *State*, 164 Ga. 467, 139 S.E. 77 (1927), summarized in Perkins, *Criminal Law*, footnote 3.

32. *Regina* v. *Bleasdale*, 2 Car. & K. 765, 175 Eng. Rep. 321 (1848), also summarized in Perkins, *Criminal Law*.

33. Perkins, *Criminal Law*, p. 642.

34. Glanville Williams, *Criminal Law: The General Part*, 2d ed. (London: Steven Sons Ltd, 1961), p. 285.

35. See Larry May, "Corporate Property Rights," *Journal of Business Ethics* 5 (1986): pp. 225–232.

36. Quoted in Perkins, *Criminal Law*, p. 642.

37. Perkins, *Criminal Law*, p. 815. It should be noted, though that for negligence to become a guilty state of mind there must be a "substantial deviation" from what a reasonable person should have done, rather than merely some deviation from this standard which is all that is required for negligence to be seen as a fault in civil law. See Perkins, pp. 754–755.

38. Peter French, "Principles of Responsibility, Shame and the Corporation," in High Curtler, ed., *Shame, Responsibility, and the Corporation*, (New York: Haven Publications, 1986), p. 45. Also see Peter French, *Collective and Corporate Responsibility*, pp. 187–202. On pages 113–114, French says that his view is not necessarily at odds with also blaming individual members of the corporation when they are also culpable.

39. French, "Principles of Responsibility," p. 46. Also see Brent Fisse and John Braithwaite, *The Impact of Publicity on Corporate Offenders* (Albany, N.Y.: State University of New York Press, 1983), especially chap. 21.

40. French, "Principles of Responsibility," p. 45.

41. Ibid., p. 44.

42. Larry May, "On Conscience," *American Philosophical Quarterly* 20 (January 1983): pp. 57–67.

43. See Normand Larendeau, "Engineering Professionalism: The Case for Corporate Ombudsmen," *Business & Professional Ethics Journal* (Fall 1982): pp. 35–47.

44. Members of Commins Engine Co. claim that their company has a conscience, and they may be right. But this would only, on my view, be something which happened because all of the relevant decision-makers in the company took into account moral issues and not only profit-making issues. For a contrasting view, see Kenneth Goodpaster and John Matthews, "Can a Corporation Have a Conscience?" *Harvard Business Review* (January–February, 1982).

45. 421 U.S. 673, 95 S. Ct. 1911.

46. Joel Feinberg, "Collective Responsibility," p. 223.

47. Virginia Held, "Can a Random Collection of Individuals be Morally Responsible?" *The Journal of Philosophy* 67 (July 23, 1970): pp. 471–481.

48. Ibid., p. 480.

49. Stanley Bates, "The Responsibility of 'Random Collections'," *Ethics* 81 (1971): p. 345.

50. For a different analysis of the conditions necessary for distributing moral responsibility among members of a collectivity, see Martin Benjamin, "Can Moral

Responsibility be Collective and Nondistributive?" *Social Theory and Practice* 4 (1976): pp. 93–106.

51. Joseph S. Ellin, "The Justice of Collective Responsibility," *University of Dayton Review* 15 (Winter 1981–1982): p. 23.

5. COMMON INTERESTS AND GROUP RIGHTS

1. Joel Feinberg, "Harm and Self-Interest," in his *Rights, Justice, and the Bounds of Liberty* (Princeton, N.J.: Princeton University Press, 1980), p. 50.

2. Ibid., p. 51.

3. Ibid., pp. 51–52.

4. Joel Feinberg, "Collective Responsibility," p. 234–235.

5. For an elaboration of this view, see Marilyn Friedman and Larry May, "Harming Women as a Group," *Social Theory and Practice* 11 (Summer 1985): pp. 218–221.

6. Owen Fiss, "Forward: The Forms of Justice," *Harvard Law Review* 93 (no. 1): pp. 1–58.

7. Owen Fiss, "Groups and the Equal Protection Clause," reprinted in *Equality and Preferential Treatment* ed. M. Cohen et al. (Princeton, N.J.: Princeton University Press, 1977), p. 125.

8. Ibid., pp. 125–126.

9. Ibid., p. 127.

10. See the first section of chapter seven for an extended discussion of the class action suit as a vehicle for alleviating or compensating groups for harmful treatment.

11. For a fascinating discussion of these issues in the American black experience, see Boris Bitker, *The Case for Black Reparations* (New York: Random House, 1973).

12. For a good illustration of the way that contemporary philosophers use the term "moral standing," see L. W. Sumner, *Abortion and Moral Theory* (Princeton, N.J.: Princeton University Press, 1981), pp. 26–33.

13. See *First National Bank of Boston, et al.,* v. *Francis X. Bellotti, etc.*, 435 U.S. 765, 55 L. Ed. 2d 707, 98 S. Ct. 1407 (1978).

14. Peter French, *Collective and Corporate Responsibility*, p. 32.

15. Ibid., pp. 44–45.

16. Ibid., p. 45.

17. See chapter two, section II.

18. Roger Pilon, "Corporations and Rights: On Treating Corporate People Justly," *Georgia Law Review* 13 (Summer 1979): pp. 1245–1370. Also see Robert Hessen, *In Defense of the Corporation* (Stanford, Calif.: Hoover Institution Press, 1979), especially chaps. 1 and 2.

19. Pilon, "Corporations and Rights," p. 1325.

20. Ibid., p. 1323 footnote 188.

21. In American law, "the corporate property is treated as belonging to the corporation not to the shareholders." Harry G. Henn, *Handbook of the Law of Corporations* (St. Paul, Minn.: West Publishing Co., 1961), p. 209.

22. See John W. Chapman, "Justice, Freedom and Property," *NOMOS XXII: Property*, p. 301 where it is claimed that the "legalized exit of shareholders through the organized trading of securities functions further to minimize the impact of externalities, in this case, externalities in the shape of corporate executives, the real owners of the modern corporations."

23. A. A. Berle and G. C. Means, *The Modern Corporation and Private Property* (New York: Macmillan, 1933), pp. 119–121.

24. Ibid.

25. In the United States, this is called the "business judgment rule." I am grateful to Thomas Donaldson for clearing up this point for me. Also see F. A. Hayek, "The Corporation in a Democratic Society: In Whose Interest Ought It and Will It Be Run?" *Studies in Philosophy, Politics and Economics* (Chicago: University of Chicago Press, 1967).

26. On the subject of minority stockholders' rights and various attempts to "freeze out" minority stockholders altogether, see Harold Friedman and Herbert S. Schlagman, *Corporate Management Guide* (New York: Matthew Bender, 1967), pp. 277–281. Also, on the way in which mergers dilute corporate control on the part of minority stockholders, see Berle and Means, *Modern Corporation and Private Property*, pp. 172–173.

27. Berle and Means list three reasons for the increased control of managers and the lessening of control by the stockholders: (1) the right to vote by proxy which separated control from stockholders and allowed managers to seize that control; (2) the disappearance of the principle that stockholders could remove directors at will; and (3) the increased statutory ability of management to act in nearly unlimited ways in behalf of the corporation. See *Modern Corporation and Private Property*, pp. 138–141.

28. Henn, *Handbook of Law*, pp. 208–209, puts the point this way: "Shareholders as such are, according to the general rule, not liable for corporate torts." Furthermore, judgments brought against the corporation as a defendant are brought only against the property of the corporation and only in very rare cases brought against the property of the shareholders (see p. 213).

29. Richard Posner, *Economic Analysis of Law* (Boston: Little, Brown and Company, 1972), p. 177.

30. Ibid., p. 178.

31. W. Michael Hoffman and James V. Fisher, "Corporate Responsibility: Property and Liability," in *Ethical Theory and Business*, ed. T. Beauchamp and N. Bowie (Englewood Cliffs, N.J.: Prentice-Hall, 1979), p. 193.

32. This is true except where "a principle shareholder strips the corporation of its assets immediately following an injury to the plaintiff." In such cases, the shareholder may be held personally liable. See Henn, *Handbook of Law*, p. 213.

33. Pierre-Joseph Proudhon, *What is Property?* trans. Benjamin Tucker, reprinted by Howard Fertig, 1966. See especially pp. 55–57 where Proudhon gives a lucid exposition and critique of the traditional liberal view of the justification of property.

34. Berle and Means, *Modern Corporation and Private Property*, pp. 355–356.

6. HARMING GROUPS

1. Henri Tajfel, *Human Groups and Social Categories* (Cambridge, Mass.: Cambridge University Press, 1981), p. 146.

2. Philip A. Goldberg, "Prejudice Against Women: Some Personality Correlates," in *Who Discriminates Against Women*, ed. Florence Denmark (Beverly Hills, Calif.: Sage, 1974), pp. 55–66.

3. Ibid., p. 64.

4. Helen Franzwa, "Female Roles in Women's Magazine Fiction, 1940–1970" in *Women: Dependent or Independent Variable?* ed. R. K. Unger (New York: Psychological Dimensions, Inc., 1975), pp. 52–53.

5. Marie Groszko and Richard Morgenstern, "Institutional Discrimination: The Case of Achievement Oriented Women in Higher Education," in *Who Discriminates Against Women?* p. 93.

6. Ibid., p. 93–94. Also see Inge Broverman, et al., "Sex Stereotypes and Clinical Judgments of Mental Health," *Journal of Consulting and Clinical Psychology* 34 (1970): pp. 1–7.

7. L. S. Fidell, "Empirical Verification of Sex Discrimination in Hiring Practices in Psychology," in *Women: Dependent or Independent Variable?* pp. 774–780.

8. "The Impact of Sexual Harassment on the Job: A Profile of the Experiences of 92 Women," in *Sexuality in Organizations*, ed. D. A. Neugarten and J. M. Shafritz (Oak Park, Ill.: Moore Publishing Co., 1980), pp. 67–72; and Catherine MacKinnon, *Sexual Harassment of Working Women* (New Haven, Conn.: Yale University Press, 1979), pp. 59–82. For a philosophical analysis, see Larry May and John C. Hughes, "Coercion in the Workplace: Sexual Offers and Sexual Threats," in *Moral Rights in the Workplace*, ed. Gertrude Ezorsky (Albany, N.Y.: State University of New York Press, 1987), pp. 115–122. Also see John C. Hughes and Larry May, "Sexual Harassment," *Social Theory and Practice* 6 (1980): pp. 249–280.

9. For more elaboration of this point, see Marilyn Friedman and Larry May, "Harming Women as a Group," *Social Theory and Practice* 11 (Summer 1985): pp. 214–218.

10. Alan Goldman, *Justice and Reverse Discrimination* (Princeton, N.J.: Princeton University Press, 1979), pp. 79–80. For a different way of criticizing Goldman, but one which aims at showing that women are harmed as a group, see Alison Jaggar's discussion note, "Relaxing the Limits of Preferential Treatment," *Social Theory and Practice* 4: pp. 227–235.

11. Alan Goldman, *Justice and Reverse Discrimination*, p. 79.

12. *First National Bank of Boston, et al., v. Francis X. Bellotti, etc.* (1978) 435 U.S. 765, 777.

13. See Thomas I. Emerson, *The System of Freedom of Expression* (New York: Random House, 1970).

14. See David A. J. Richards, "The Moral Theory of Free Speech and Obscenity Law," in *Freedom of Speech*, ed. Fred R. Berger (Belmont, Calif.: Wadsworth Publishing Co., 1980), pp. 99–127.

15. See Marilyn Friedman, "Autonomy and the Split-Level Self," *Southern Journal of Philosophy* 24 (Spring 1986): pp. 19–35.

16. 435 U.S. 824.

17. See 435 U.S. 824 where Justice Rehnquist argues explicitly for this conclusion.

18. See *NAACP* v. *Alabama ex rel. Patterson*, 357 U.S. 449 (1958), and *NAACP* v. *Button*, 371 U.S. 415 (1963) where the Supreme Court first grappled with these issues. I will analyze these cases in more detail in chapter seven, section II.

19. See T. M. Scanlon, Jr., "Freedom of Expression and Categories of Expression," *University of Pittsburgh Law Review* 40 (1979). Also see T. M. Scanlon, Jr., "A Theory of Freedom of Expression," *Philosophy and Public Affairs* 1 (Winter 1972): pp. 204–226.

20. Alexander Meiklejohn, "The First Amendment is an Absolute," *1961 Supreme Court Review*, pp. 245–266, reprinted in *Freedom of Expression: A Collection of Best Writings*, ed. Kent Middleton and Roy S. Mersky (Buffalo, N.Y.: William S. Hein and Co., 1981), p. 75.

21. Edwin Rome and William H. Roberts, *Corporate and Commercial Free Speech* (Westport, Conn.: Greenwood Press, 1985), p. 237.

22. Emerson, *System of Freedom of Expression*, chap. 1.

23. See Justice White's dissent in *Bellotti*, 435 U.S. 809–812.

24. 435 U.S. 809.

25. For an interesting analysis of whether the *Bellotti* case is inconsistent with current restrictions on corporate expression during federal elections, see Charles R. O'Kelley, Jr., "The Constitutional Rights of Corporations Revisited: Social and Political Expression and the Corporation after *First National Bank* v. *Bellotti*," *Georgetown Law Review* 67 (1979): pp. 1375–1382.

26. For a spirited defense, on slightly different grounds, of the thesis presented here, see Patricia Werhane, *Persons, Rights, and Corporations* (Englewood Cliffs, N.J.: Prentice-Hall, 1985), pp. 63–64.

7. JUSTICE FOR GROUPS

1. Marshall Breger, "Legal Aid for the Poor: A Conceptual Analysis," *North Carolina Law Review* 60 (1982): pp. 282–297.

2. Departments of Labor, and Health, Education, and Welfare, and related agencies, *Appropriations for Fiscal Year 1971: Hearings on 18515*, 91st Congress (Washington, D.C.: Government Printing Office, 1970), part 2, p. 534.

3. L. Goodman and M. Walters, *The Legal Services Program: Resource Distribution and the Low Income Population* (1975), quoted in C. Bellow and J. Kettleson, "From Ethics to Politics: Confronting Scarcity and Fairness in Public Interest Practice," *Boston University Law Review* 58 (1978): p. 342 note 26.

4. Breger, "Legal Aid for Poor," p. 292.

5. Ibid., p. 289.

6. Ibid., p. 289 note 39.

7. Henry Shue, *Basic Rights* (Princeton, N.J.: Princeton University Press, 1980), pp. 22–34.

8. As Breger notes, John Rawls makes a similar distinction between primary and secondary goods ("Legal Aid for Poor," p. 293).

9. James Childress, "Who Shall Live When Not All Can Live?" *Soundings* 53 (1970): pp. 347–354.

10. Ronald Dworkin, *Taking Rights Seriously* (Cambridge, Mass.: Harvard University Press, 1977), p. 227.

11. Childress, "Who Shall Live?" pp. 348–350.

12. Breger, "Legal Aid for Poor," p. 292.

13. Ibid., pp. 287, 295, 340, and 344.

14. See John M. Taurek, "Should the Numbers Count?" *Philosophy and Public Affairs* 6 (1977): p. 293.

15. Derek Parfit, responding to Taurek's article, argues that, to be at all defensible, one must take this position. See "Innumerate Ethics," *Philosophy and Public Affairs* 7 (1978): p. 285.

16. Ibid., p. 301.

17. Breger, "Legal Aid for Poor," p. 286.

18. Ibid., p. 357.

19. Federal Rules of Civil Procedure #23, advisory committee note.

20. *Halderman* v. *Pennhurst State School and Hospital*, 612 F.2d 84, 88–89 (3rd Cir. 1979).

21. Ibid., pp. 90, 116. On this point, see D. Bell, "Serving Two Masters: Integration Ideals and Client Interests in School Desegregation Litigation," *Yale Law Journal* 85 (1976): pp. 482–487.

22. See D. Rhode, "Class Conflicts in Class Actions," *Stanford Law Review* 34 (1982): pp. 1211–1212.

23. *Regents of the University of California* v. *Bakke*, 438 U.S. 265 (1978).

24. Some economists have argued that the difficulty in defining poverty is reason for regarding it as having little descriptive meaning. See Mollie Orshansky, "How Poverty is Measured," *Monthly Labor Review* (February 1969): p. 37. However, Amartya Sen argues that poverty can be defined on the basis of standards measuring minimum needs, that is, what is necessary to escape the kind of economic deprivation that leads to hunger and starvation. See Amartya Sen, *Poverty and Famines: An Essay on Entitlement and Deprivation* (New York: Oxford University Press, 1981), pp. 24–38. Although one need not be a member of the group of poor people throughout one's whole life in the way that members of other disadvantaged groups (for example, women or blacks) are, at any given time it is possible to determine that a person is unable to meet minimum needs. Welfare officials have been making these calculations for some time, and most social scientists and economists now recognize the minimum needs standard in identifying the poor.

25. Because the poor often face institutions as legal opponents, their problems are more difficult to solve that those raised in a nonpoor person's disputes, which are usually private. See S. Stumpf, "Law and Poverty: A Political Perspective," *University of Wisconsin Law Review* 1968: pp. 698–701.

26. Breger, "Legal Aid for Poor," pp. 287–288.

27. The legal historian Stephen Yeazell contends that "seventeenth century group litigation is not about the legal rights of aggrieved individuals, but about the incidents of status flowing from membership in an agricultural community not yet part of a market economy." See his "Group Litigation and Social Context: Toward

a History of the Class Action Suit," *Columbia University Law Review* 77 (1977): p. 871. See also his essay, "From Group Litigation to Class Action, Part I: The Industrialization of Group Litigation," *UCLA Law Review* 27 (1980): pp. 517–520.

28. *NAACP* v. *Alabama* (1958) 357 U.S. 458–459.

29. Ibid., p. 460.

30. Ibid., p. 462.

31. *NAACP* v. *Button* (1963) 371 U.S. 428–431.

32. Ibid., p. 444.

33. Ibid., p. 445.

34. Ibid., p. 444.

35. For further support, see Alan Gewirth's defense of the needs of the disadvantaged to special protection and aid by the courts, "Civil Liberties as Effective Powers," reprinted in his *Human Rights* (Chicago: University of Chicago Press, 1982), pp. 310–328.

CONCLUSION

1. John Rawls, *A Theory of Justice* (Cambridge, Mass.: Harvard University Press, 1971), p. 8.

2. Ibid., p. 521.

3. See Alisdair MacIntyre, *After Virtue* (Notre Dame, Ind.: University of Notre Dame Press, 1981), chaps. 11 and 12.

4. See the sections on Anglo-Saxon law in Theodore F. T. Plucknett, *A Concise History of the Common Law*, 5th ed. (Boston: Little, Brown and Co., 1956), specifically p. 9.

5. See Robert Nozick's discussion of the libertarian constraints on morality in *Anarchy State and Utopia* (New York: Basic Books, 1974), as reprinted in *Liberalism and its Critics*, ed. Michael Sandel (New York: New York University Press, 1984), p. 105–106.

Index